GOLF
The Mind Factor

GOLF
The Mind Factor

DARREN CLARKE
with Dr Karl Morris

HODDER &
STOUGHTON

Copyright ©2005 by Darren Clarke and Karl Morris

First published in Great Britain in 2005 by Hodder & Stoughton

A division of Hodder Headline

The right of Darren Clarke and Karl Morris to be identified as the Authors of the Work has been asserted by them in accordance with the Copyright, Designs and Patents Act 1988.

A Hodder & Stoughton Book

1

A CIP catalogue record for this title is available from the British Library

Hardback ISBN 0340 896264
Trade paperback ISBN 0340 840633

Typeset in Officina Serif and Sans Serif by Eric Drewery Design

Printed and bound by
Bath Press Ltd, Lower Bristol Road, Bath BA2 3BL

Hodder Headline's policy is to use papers that are neutral, renewable and recyclable products and made from wood grown in sustainable forests. The logging and manufacturing processes are expected to conform to the environmental regulations of the country of origin.

Hodder & Stoughton Ltd
A division of Hodder Headline
338 Euston Road
London NW1 3BH

*To all the talented players who know they can do it,
but struggle to control their inner thoughts.*

Contents

CONTENTS

Acknowledgements

I would like to thank Dr Karl Morris for giving me the benefit of his vast experience in the field of sports psychology. His knowledge has been truly transformational and it is for this reason that I felt I should share with readers, golfers and indeed non-golfers, his extraordinary insights and their effect on my game and my career. Working with Karl was a voyage of discovery, which introduced me to new and fascinating aspects of the game of golf.

I should like to mention sports journalist Martin Hardy, who was particularly helpful in putting my thoughts into words. My thanks too to Peter Dennison who gave me my first introduction into the world of psychology.

The excellent illustrations in this book by Graham Gaches also deserve praise for their clarity.

Roddy Bloomfield at Hodder & Stoughton guided Karl and me in shaping and structuring this book and we were happy to draw on his expertise in sports publishing. Maybe in return his golf will improve!

Lastly, and most importantly, I would like to express fondest thanks to my wife and family, who give added value to everything I achieve.

Darren Clarke

Photographic acknowledgements
The author and publisher would like to thank the following for permission to reproduce photographs:
Empics, Getty Images, Phil Sheldon Golf Picture Library

Introduction:
Mind over matter

Darren Clarke: It was Arnold Palmer who said golf is 20 per cent physical and 80 per cent mental. I absolutely agree with the great man. You can have the greatest technique, the greatest swing and the sweetest putting stroke in the world, but you will never play the golf that you're capable of if you have a poor mental approach.

When I was 16 and had already decided I wanted to be a golf professional, I was introduced to the mental side of golf by the psychologist Peter Dennison in Portadown. After meeting him, I became determined to be not just an ordinary golf professional but a successful tournament winner. Since that time, I have thought a great deal about my mental approach to all aspects of the game and am constantly looking to improve in this area. I am indebted to the teachings of Dr Karl Morris, a former professional golfer turned sports psychologist, who now works with multiple top sportsmen such as Paul McGinley and Graeme McDowell in golf, Michael Vaughan in cricket, and Jimmy White in snooker. His work is a combination of extensive research, development, and the inevitable trial and error. I know no one who has helped me better to unravel some of the mysteries of the mind as they relate to golf, and I am certain that his advice and guidance can help you enormously with your game, whatever your current level or standard of play.

Karl Morris: Darren is a massively talented professional with an in-depth understanding of the key role played by the mind in professional golf. When we decided to write this book together, we felt that it could be of enormous value to the amateur golfer anxious to improve his handicap, or maybe simply to recapture some lost enjoyment from the game. We will describe in simple terms the role of the mind as it relates to the game of golf. You will have a number of keys you can apply to your game straightaway. We are convinced that you will be both surprised and delighted with the results.

Darren: My role in the book is to share with you some of my own golfing experiences and the challenges I have faced. I have no doubt you will be able to relate to these experiences whether you play the game at the highest level or are just a keen club golfer. As human beings, we all get nervous; we all need to focus our concentration; we all hit bad shots; we all need to get over the inevitable disappointments the game brings to us. These are just some of the common problems we face, whether we are amateurs or professionals.

Karl: My passion for the past 10 years or so has been to demystify sports psychology and to take it from being an academic minefield of complexity to a useable and practical discipline. You don't have to read this book from cover to cover, although some of you may find that useful. All the most common challenges we face in golf are discussed here. Feel free to home in on whatever you consider your own particular area of interest. But I would highly recommend you to focus on no more than a couple of issues at any one time as you develop your mental game.

Darren: I think that many golfers believe the secret of good golf is to acquire a perfect swing, and to play and practise as much as you possibly can. I would be the last person to say that these objectives are unimportant, but they aren't the whole story. You won't become the golfer that you're capable of being unless you address, and work with, the mind factor. One thing I'm sure of is that what goes on in a golfer's head determines his score even more than the technical aspects. I have found that Karl has a clarity and simplicity in his approach to understanding the mental game, and that he can help you as much as he continues to help me.

Playing great golf:
The art of effective
preparation

Darren: I was a pretty good amateur, winning quite a few tournaments, and a lot of my initial success was down to the work I put in on the mental side. Few others were doing anything similar at that time, but it was clear to me that, whether you are a pro or an amateur, you're always looking to have a bit of an edge over the opposition. That idea put me on the trail of working on the negative thought processes that invade a golfer's mind. Many people don't rate the mental side of the game highly, but a little bit of work and patience in this area can only help; it can't make a golfer worse in any way. Improvement is the only by-product if the mind is strong, determined and focused.

Golfers on tour can all play the game, otherwise we wouldn't be where we are. That side of things is sorted for professionals. But in the amateur game, when people don't play that often, players facing difficult shots may get very anxious over them. They often talk themselves out of hitting a good shot before they've even attempted it.

Visualising things is massively important. If you don't visualise, then you allow other negative thoughts to enter your head. Not visualising is almost like having a satellite navigation system in your car, but not entering your destination into it. The machinery can only work if you put everything in there. You can't sit in your car wondering what's happening to the engine all the time. In golf if you do that, you're not playing the game any more, you're just playing golf swing.

When I play poorly I think about my golf swing, the mechanics and technique. But when I'm just thinking about these, then I have no focus on my target. All I'm concerned about is where the club needs to be to strike the ball where I want it to go. But if I'm not picking my target, I might as well just start hitting the ball into the next field, because I am not focusing my brain on where I want it to go.

It's very difficult at times to catch myself, and force myself to get out of the mechanical and technical side of the game and more into the mental side. Indeed, I have performed at my best when I have not been thinking about anything at all! This seems a strange thing to say, but if my mind is clear and all I see is the target, club back, club through, then invariably the ball goes towards it. Whenever I'm thinking about technique, the ball disappears at all kinds of funny angles – and I mean funny peculiar, not funny ha-ha!

Nobody can make a perfect swing time after time after time. On tour we all strive to be technically perfect, to try to hit perfect shots all the time, but the game doesn't work that way. The fact is, we think about the mechanics more than we should. It almost seems mandatory on tour that you work on your technique. But the minute you step out on the first tee you have to forget about it. That's the hard part.

Be prepared!

My preparation, physical, technical and mental, starts way before first tee-off on Thursday. Thanks to the efforts of fitness expert Steve Hampson and body conditioner John Newton, I am now in the best physical shape of my career, and one of the benefits has been that I feel fit in mind as well as in body.

It has been said of me that my idea of the perfect day off is a round of golf, but my normal practice regime starts on the Tuesday. I either play nine holes or 18 depending on how and where I am, how well I know the course, how I'm feeling, and how much I need to work on things. If I've played the course before, I'm a little bit more at ease because I know where I'm going and what I'll be doing to get the best possible result. If you know where the locker rooms are, where registration is, and all those little things, that makes preparation just that little bit easier.

I practise for an hour to 90 minutes, incorporating a variation of hitting balls, chipping and putting, but probably more putting than anything else. I try to get used to the speed of the greens as much as I can because they do vary from event to event. Being confident on the greens is a major part of scoring the right numbers.

NUGGET

> Keeping practice competitive guards against the possibility of just doing things for the sake of them. One game involves using just one ball rather than the collection you would have in normal practice. It's what Karl calls Par 18 – using one ball to chip up and hole out from nine different spots, and each one is a par two. You chip up and hole out and go all the way round. Suddenly there's some competition involved, wagers are struck, such as paying for dinner or the wine. Even though you're having some fun, you finish up training your mind as well as your body and technique. As a consequence, the success rates for up and downs improve.

Wednesday is pro-am day. Normally I like to play early, so I get to the course a good hour before, play 18 and look round for any changes to the course because, although it may be the same stretch of terrain, there are some subtle and some not-so-subtle alterations that are introduced year after year. I also check the rough to see if it's thicker on one side of the fairway than the other, and also which sides of any green you can afford to miss on to give you a better chance of getting up and down.

My caddie Billy Foster will put a couple of tee pegs in the green to indicate where the pins will be during tournament rounds, because invariably they use the same positions – not always in the same order, but the same hole locations. Basically, I'm just trying to get a feel for the course. Afterwards I'll hit some balls for a while, but if I'm swinging OK, I'll just chip and putt.

If I have a 7.30 tee-time on Thursday, I will be up at 4.30 and try to be in the gym at 4.45 for 45 minutes when I do some stretching and loosen up. I arrive at the golf course 90 minutes before my tee off, try to grab a bit of a healthy breakfast, and then warm up. This is when I start thinking about what I'm trying to achieve that day. Then I have last-minute checks on my swing, normally conducted by my caddie Billy Foster, who has been with me so long he knows my swing very well indeed.

Then I go through my bag, lob wedge, sand wedge, pitching wedge, then to a nine iron, seven, five, three, five wood, three wood, driver. If I'm struggling with any of those I'll go back to them after the routine and hit a few more. I prefer to hit balls first, and then chip and putt for 40 minutes afterwards, but it depends on the location of both practice areas in relation to the first tee.

The important thing now is to believe in what I'm doing and trust in myself, which might not always be easy if I haven't been hitting the ball great on the range. The worst pre-round practice session I have ever had was in Monte Carlo in 1992. I was duffing it, shanking it, thinning it, topping it, and if I was doing anything right, I was unaware of it. I went out on to the golf course with possibly the least expectation I had ever had – and shot 60. I had no idea what happened. I just went out and hit the ball, found it, hit it again and putted, and signed for a 60. Maybe the moral for me is right there: I probably shoot better when my expectation levels are not as high.

That nervous feeling

I'm always a little bit nervous before any competitive round. I think it was Jack Nicklaus who said: 'If you're not shaking on the last green when you're trying to win a golf tournament then there's something wrong with you.' Nervousness is a feeling, and if you haven't got certain feelings going through your body then you are dead. What matters is the label we put on it. It's like Tiger Woods said after a shootout with Phil Mickelson: 'If you are not feeling things like I was when going head to head with Mickelson, then you are not alive.'

Nervousness is energy, it means you're ready to play. You should almost welcome it because, as Big Jack used to say: 'Give me that feeling on the back nine of a major.' But occasionally this game does things you don't expect. Greg Norman has been one of the greatest players ever, and he was my hero growing up. But sometimes the game gets away from you, no matter how mentally strong you are, it just doesn't go for you. It is as simple as that. When Nick Faldo went head to head with Norman in 1996 at the US Masters, that was one of those occasions. That was a day when it got away from Norman, and no matter what he tried to do, it didn't work. It was a very unfortunate day for him, although Nick Faldo played great golf because any 67 is fantastic at Augusta. Greg's game just got away from him, and the harder he tried, the worse it got. It's sad because he deserved to win at Augusta with the game that he normally had. But I think you can learn a lot more about a person in defeat than you can in victory. Greg Norman in that Press Conference afterwards was unbelievable. A lot of other people would not have acted so graciously. There was nothing he could do about the way Faldo was playing, because if that day proved one thing it was that we are in control of our own destiny and that's all.

The strongest players are the best players, and all they do is the best they can, given the ability they have. They forget about everybody else. If you do that then you can walk off with your head held high. If however you let your game be determined by how somebody else is playing, that's when you start having trouble.

Even when it's a head-to-head situation in a stroke-play format, if it comes down to just two of you in contention then you have played well enough to get into that position, so it's unwise to worry about what the other player is doing. You must try not to get ahead of yourself and press too hard.

One of my biggest problems has always been expectations. Because I know how I can play and how I can hit the ball, I go out with expectations of shooting 57–58, whatever. I'm hitting it so well on the range, and then I go out and hit one or two bad shots early, and I start asking myself where it's gone wrong – and end up shooting 71–72 because my expectations were so high. It's much better to go on a golf course with no expectations, as my 60 in Monte Carlo proves. Just go out and play rather than think you are going to play great.

It's like you've put a number in your mind, and if your first four holes don't match that number then you go chasing it. Going out with a 'let's see what happens' frame of mind is the equivalent of not having expectations. Let's see what happens, then you can deal with playing awful. Let's see what happens, and if you get on a roll then you can go with it and score –9 –10. There have been loads of times when I have flushed it in practice and not produced in the tournament, come nowhere near; and other times when on the range I couldn't hit the proverbial cow's backside with a banjo, and then flushed it on the course.

There was a period a couple of years ago at the start of the year when I could hit every shot to order. Billy Foster could call a four-yard draw or a two-yard fade, low punch, rising draw, high soft cut, and on the range I could hit every shot he called right on to the target. Yet as soon as I got on the course I could not do it. I'd try to hit one shot, fail, and I'd start asking myself: 'Where's my swing gone?' I was being counter-productive. Then I'd start missing greens from the middle of the fairway, and after thinking I'd be getting a birdie I'd bogey instead and walk off wondering how on earth had I just done that. This would force me to go to the next hole and start chasing the flag as opposed to staying on the correct side of the hole.

One of my best ball-striking rounds ever was at the US Open at Olympia Fields in 2003. I hit it great from tee to green all week, but just didn't return the kind of scores I should have done. It is almost more enjoyable to play poorly but think well and produce a score, than it is just to hit the ball great and score well. I said almost! But to play poorly, think well, and score well is the difference between a good player and a great one.

I'd love to say that my thought processes were the same for a regular tournament as for a major, but they do alter even though they shouldn't. There's more build-up to a major, and therefore more time to think, but I'm at the stage of my career when I want to win one, and I have been close a couple of times. I want to get myself in a position where I can challenge for one and win one, and then take it on from there.

The goal for me at the moment is getting myself into the position where I can challenge. I have been there before so I do know what it's like, I know what to expect. Solid golf wins Major Championships, not just spectacular birdies, but unfortunately I don't see the game of golf as one where you play for pars. That's the way I look at it. So it's hard for me to realise sometimes that pin-high, 30ft right is a good shot. It's one of my failings at times which I have to admit to. Without doubt, though, I am learning to come up with the ingredients that Major winners undoubtedly possess.

I try to be more relaxed going into Majors, I try to prepare myself as well as I can, but more than ever I have that desire and determination to win one, so it's hard to control my emotions. If I let my desire get in front of what I need to do to get there, then that causes problems because I want victory too much.

Levels of intensity

Karl tells me that my intensity would be fine if I was a rugby player, because some of that energy could be released out on the pitch with the physical nature of the game. However, this doesn't work with golf. You can't hit anybody with a crunching tackle, or run harder and chase the ball to release your pent-up emotion. You can't make the golf ball go in the hole. What you have to do is keep the desire within a calm framework. Calm is key.

This is what I try to take with me into the Majors. I like to get to a championship venue at least one day earlier than normal because the courses are usually tougher than we're used to. In US Opens and US PGAs, for example, the rough is invariably thicker so you pay a huge premium for missing the fairways. That takes some getting used to, as do rock-hard greens. The British Open venues are not too bad. I have played them all and know most of them quite well. They can't really change a links course much because a links course is a links course. As for Augusta, there's always a new trick here or there, always a new pin they throw at us that we don't know. If the greens are slow on practice days, you might get to the course on Thursday morning, hit into the first green, and watch your ball jump 30 feet in the air, and realise they have sucked all the water out of them. That's the thing about Augusta, you never know what the course is going to be like, particularly what the greens are going to have in store for you, until you've played the first hole on Thursday morning. I love Augusta for what it is, and the fact that it is totally different from anywhere else. If they have good weather they can throw all sorts of surprises at us and they delight in doing exactly that.

My demeanour in the past has depended on how I was hitting the ball. If I was hitting it well then I'd be relaxed. If not, then I'm probably the last person you would want to be around. But with the progress I've made with Karl this has improved markedly over the last couple of years.

I can be my own worst enemy and get annoyed with myself too easily because I know how good my good is and how bad my bad is. It annoys me because I know how well I can play, and when I don't get anywhere near it that's when I get frustrated and, as a consequence, mentally on edge.

Karl: Darren is massively gifted as a golfer, but he does have to work at the mental side. There are some golfers who haven't been gifted with half as much talent but are stronger mentally, and it balances out. Nick Faldo was both gifted in his precision and mentally strong. Woods was working on the mental side when he was 12, Faldo in the early 1980s when he never admitted it to anybody.

Darren: There's always a hint of trepidation as you walk on to the first tee at a major championship. With me it's sometimes a little more so if I'm not hitting the ball how I want to, and less so if the ball flight is under control.

I normally couldn't care less who I'm paired with. I get on with 99.9 per cent of the players, so I'm not worried who I'm going to be with for the next five hours. If I'm to perform the way I want to, then I have to shut everything out as soon as I hit the first tee. If I don't or can't do that, then I'm not in the right frame of mind to play golf. If I'm not in the right frame of mind, then I'm beating my head against a brick wall because my focus is not where it should be.

To be honest, the only thing I think about when I am on the first tee is how do I get this thing on the fairway. At the US Open, you take whatever club you can just to get the ball on the fairway. The better I am playing, the fewer swing thoughts I have. At the World Golf Championship, which I won in 2003, I had one swing thought for all four rounds and that was rhythm, all week. There was nothing else. I swung smoothly, walked slowly between shots, and remained calm throughout. We watched a video afterwards and it was weird because I was just ambling around, even in the last round. When I play well I stroll, smoke my cigar, have a nice time, and worry about nothing. When I'm not playing well, I sprint to the ball, swing quick, hit it quick and I'm never into my target.

I've worked a lot with Karl on the pace I walk at between shots. When I'm ambling, I'm fine, but when I walk quickly, the rhythm in the golf swing disappears. If you watch me in the pressurised atmosphere of the Ryder Cup – and there have been a few where I have played reasonably well – I'm usually very slow and deliberate, and don't rush anything. I take my time, and the benefits come with it.

Tiger says he learns something from every round of golf he plays, and usually when I am playing well I learn something. When I'm not playing well, I'm too quick to blame it on technique. When I analyse a game afterwards I look for the technical mistakes more than the mental ones, yet I make more mental ones than technical ones.

Producing a good score doesn't always mean shooting 62–63. A 70 when I'm not on my game is every bit as gratifying as a low score. You may win tournaments, but very few people have four fantastic rounds to do that. It doesn't happen. You may have three rounds when you hit the ball great and score really well, but not four. On the one off day, if you can turn a 73 into a 69, then that's how you win tournaments. Last year in the Visa Taheiyo, I played great for the first 45 holes, and then I ground it out for the rest of it. My short game kept me going, and that's what took me first past the finishing post.

People I talk to, friends or amateur pro-am partners, think you win the game through ball-striking and ball-striking alone. But it's a far cry from that. Usually the best short game and best mental game wins at the end of the week. You can't have one without the other.

Karl: Normally we're never able to judge the mental game properly because we have nothing to score it by. However, we have set up a game where you can score a maximum of 40 mental points over the course of a four-round tournament. So every day the aim has to be to have a 10 'mental day'. This way you have some method of judging your improvement, but without this kind of feedback it's difficult to chart your progress or to know what to work on.

Darren: I don't know how or why I ever came up with this theory, but it was something that followed Ben Hogan's saying that he only ever hit three perfect shots. As a youngster, when I was in bed and before I got to sleep, I would go through my round, and I would have to make the good things from the day outnumber the bad things. If I didn't outnumber the bad things by six I had had a poor day.

I would go through every shot, drive, iron, chip or putt, and I'd just go with either the good or bad shots, and forget the average ones. If I didn't have six more good shots than bad ones, then there was something I had to work on. I started doing this when I was 15 and now and again I still do it.

You never stop learning, tinkering, or trying to improve a little. If things aren't going quite as well as you would like then you must try to find a remedy. But one thing is for sure, it's what goes on inside a golfer's head that determines his score, far more than the technical aspect.

Effective coaching: Making the most of your lessons

Darren: John Garner was my first coach before I played my way into the Irish Boys team. Next I went to Howard Bennett, a lovely man. Then I turned professional and went to Bob Torrance, Pete Cowen, Butch Harmon, Pete Cowen, Butch Harmon, and back to Pete Cowen again. Let's just say I've had an on-off relationship with my last two coaches but, like all the others, they are excellent in their own way.

There are two types of players that coaches have to deal with: technical and feel. I would probably put myself on the 'feel' side of that divide because I don't want to know too much about what's going on technically.

I grew up in Northern Ireland playing my golf in Dungannon initially, and then Portrush. When you're playing on a cold December morning and it's almost freezing, as well as blowing 50 mph, then you can almost throw the technical aspect of the game away as you have to rely on your imagination and feel. A lot of the amateur tournaments I played in as I grew up were on some of the oldest and best links courses in the world, courses where you had to hit the ball very low. Not that you don't have to on some American courses, but on links you have to do it that little bit more. Nowadays I'm always aware of having too much technical information, yet whenever I've struggled that's the area I go to – which means my mind gets even more messed up than it was to start with! Coaches always want to help us, and sometimes I find myself going for technical answers when that hasn't been the cause of the problem. I go looking for answers when instead I should just carry on working, keep my head down, and simply wait for the results to come through. It's imperative to work with a coach who understands you and your style of learning. Keeping things simple and easy to understand is the hallmark of an effective coach. Be aware of information overload.

Patience is definitely not one of my virtues, and that's probably because I crave success, occasionally perhaps too much. Some people may look at my career and consider that I have been reasonably successful, but I'm not one of them. I'd describe it as stunningly average! I am my worst critic anyway, but I believe my best golf is yet to come. Now that I'm a little bit older I am getting a bit wiser.

The second time I shot 60 in a tournament was at the K-Club when I was in a world of my own. I had no swing thoughts. I had one or two practice swings, stood up to the ball, looked at my target, took the club back and through, and the ball went to six feet. That was it. With two holes to go I realised a 59 was on. On 17 I hit three iron and by then I'd slightly come out of where I'd been all day. Then I started thinking about shooting 59 on one of the most difficult courses we play on all year. Perfect three iron, and then a nine iron to 15 feet right of the flag. Over the putt I was back into the zone, and I hit the purest putt. It was only going one place and then, six inches from the hole, it went a hair right and lipped out. I had done everything I could possibly do, but for whatever reason it didn't go in.

Then I was in between clubs after my drive on the last, and came up 30 feet short. I knew I had to hole it for 59 and forced it a little, and pulled it, so from halfway I knew it wasn't going in. It went five feet past, and I did well to hole the one coming back for 60. I remember standing over the second putt, and I was so deflated that I'd let the chance go to shoot 59. I said to myself, 'Whatever you do, don't miss this, otherwise it's a 61.' I remember coming off the course having just shot 60, and I was really down on myself because I hadn't shot 59 and become the first player in Europe to do it.

I keep a little black book with notes and things from the technical side, and that's something I would recommend that you do with your own coach. I'm not embarrassed to ask players if I see them do something I'm interested in. But the mental side is something we all keep close to our chests, it's not usually a topic of general conversation.

The short game

One of the most frequently asked questions that comes to my website (www.darrenclarke.com) is about practice. When people ask what are the three main things they should practise to improve, I always reply, 'First, short game; second, short game; third, short game.'

It didn't take me long to realise that the part of my game that wasn't as good as it could be was the short game. Hence I had to do a lot of work on it, and still do. It wasn't just the short game only, but the mental game it was aligned to. Your wedges and your putter are the scoring clubs, and you have to score with those. They can get you out of jail a lot of times.

It's obviously much easier to hit a wedge close than it is a three iron, so your target should be a lot smaller, a lot narrower, with the short irons. Occasionally I've tended to get that a little bit mixed up. I'd be going at the flag, taking on impossible shots with my long irons, as opposed to zeroing in on my target with my short irons, and that doesn't lead to good scoring. Successful professional golf is not about how well you strike it, how beautiful a flight the ball goes on, it's simply how many shots you take to get it into the hole.

If you are not mentally strong you're going to make mistakes and turn your 69s into 72s instead of turning your 72s into 69s. No matter how good you are, you're going to beat your head against a brick wall all day long if you think you're going to win tournaments doing that. Turning three shots into two is the hallmark of a truly great player. And there's a knock-on effect, because if the confidence is there with the short game, you can unleash the long game.

The professional game works from the green backwards. If you're putting well, then you won't mind if you're chipping to six feet. If you're chipping well, you won't mind if you miss a green with a six iron because you're going to chip to six feet and then hole it. If your iron play is good, it doesn't really matter if you miss the green. You still have to drive well these days because of the rough and the way they prepare it, but the premium is always going to be on the short game.

Sometimes you have to accept your punishment and try to get the ball into the hole in as few shots as possible. You have to figure out the percentages to limit the damage. Billy Foster is very sensible, he knows me very well, knows how I want to play, and knows what I want to do. And he has stopped me a few times from going for shots I wanted to. He will put his hand over a three wood and won't let me take it out. He'll lie on top of the bag at times before he'll let me have it, so a lot of the way I play the golf course is down to him. It's mutual, obviously, because I always have the last say, but if I mess it up then I know I'm going to hear 'I told you so' when we walk down the fairway.

We've had a few disagreements. A couple of years ago I was on the last hole, having just made bogey on the hole before. I was doing reasonably OK, but he said he wanted me to hit a three wood, and I told him to give me the driver.

'No.'

'Give me the bloody driver.'

'No.'

'Give me the ******* driver!'

He said, 'Fine, OK, hit it.'

I hit it into the bunker and finished up making double bogey. Then I turned to Billy and said, 'What on earth did you give me the driver for?'

Overall, I trust Billy implicitly. He's very level-headed, not like me at all. He always looks at the bigger picture and always keeps calm, because he realises that an emotional caddie is a recipe for disaster.

Pre-shot routines

One thing Billy rarely has to remind me about is my pre-shot routine. One of the biggest mistakes amateurs make is not having a pre-shot routine. If you watch a professional you will see he always goes through one. It takes mental discipline to go through your routine each time, but it's massively important. I see so many amateurs get up over the ball, stand there, and not know what they're doing. All they say to themselves is, 'I don't want to hit it in the water, just get it over the water.' They end up thinking so much about the water that the ball is never going to go anywhere else.

We professionals have the same thoughts if we allow them to creep into our minds, but that's why we have a pre-shot routine. We mimic what we're going to do over the ball, what swing we're going to make, where we want to see the ball in the air, what shape it's going to go into the green, where it's going to land and where it's going to finish. Amateurs tend to stand up there and hit it without doing any of that whatsoever. I'm not saying this will turn a 24 handicapper into a scratch player throughout a season, but it will improve him. If players start thinking about what they want to do rather than what they don't want to do, it makes a massive difference.

NUGGET

As Karl has often told me, the brain cannot process a negative. So if I say 'the dog is not chasing the cat,' you will probably have made some kind of picture of a dog chasing a cat to make sense of the words. In the same way, if we are telling ourselves to keep away from the trouble, we are painting pictures in our mind of the very thing that we want to avoid.

Pressure is pressure whatever your handicap; if you have the chance to win the monthly medal you still need to have a routine. Why does a fireman go through the fire drill every day? It doesn't matter whether it's a chip-pan fire or the entire street burning down, he does it so that he can do under pressure the same thing that he's been practising before.

I'm not advocating slow play, but I've known occasions when amateurs who have been watching a lot of golf on television think they should ape what they've seen. They have two practice swings behind the ball, two to the side, put the clubs across their hips and then across their shoulders, check this, check that – but by the time it comes to hit the ball they don't know what they're supposed to be doing. Most pros stand to the side and take one practice shot, stand behind the ball, visualise the shot and then get over it and hit it. It's a consistent routine which would definitely help amateurs. Most amateurs don't think before they get to the ball. They whip the club out of the bag, get over it and then start thinking. That's the easiest way to a muddled mind.

Where a pre-shot routine would help the amateur every time is over those four-foot putts. So many amateurs approach believing they're going to miss, as opposed to thinking they will hole them. Amateurs don't like four-footers, whereas professionals, although they don't make them all, are pretty good at them. We do drills, for instance we'll do 50 in a row of having to hole from four feet. I tell myself I have to hole them all or start again if I miss. It doesn't half concentrate the mind especially when you get over 30. You get into a routine of knocking them in. Amateurs don't have time to do that sort of thing, but if they could get themselves into a routine it would make such a difference to their scores.

All you have to do when you get on the green is think you are a good putter - whether you are or not is irrelevant. That way you have more chance of holing as opposed to saying, 'Oh no, not another four-footer. I don't want to roll this one past, but I don't want to look a pussy and leave it three feet short.' That's the way most amateurs think. Just think you're going to hole it, because if you expect to hit a bad shot then invariably you will. If you hit a good one it's a fluke! You have more chance of hitting a good one if you think you're going to hit a good one. It's the same on the greens.

Another huge aspect to golf is breathing. Half the amateurs I see are going blue in the face before they hit the ball, and that's a recipe for disaster. Golfers tend to think that concentrating on breathing is something only pregnant women do. It's not. If you grab a golf club and keep hold of it and then tell an amateur to practise a shot, I would say 99 per cent of them would breathe in, hold their breath and then start strangling the grip, holding it so tight because they're holding their breath. That naturally tightens up your muscles, and your brain starts asking, 'What's going on?' That sends messages to tighten up the muscles more because you're expecting something bad to happen. If you took a deep breath and then exhaled, and then took the club back just as you were finishing exhaling, it would make a big difference. The tempo and rhythm of the swing would be completely different and much improved. When you are breathing out you're actually clearing your mind of a lot of garbage anyway.

Mental strength

I would have to say that of the current bunch of players, Tiger Woods is mentally stronger than any of us. Whether he's playing fantastic golf or poor golf, he gives 110 per cent every time he goes on the course. He gets perturbed as we all do from time to time, but his mind is right back on it the next time he has to hit the ball. He went through a swing change in 2004 when he wasn't playing his best, and he'd get annoyed with himself, but he'd still grind it out. He ground it out every time, and scored as well as he could. People called it a slump but he still won five million dollars that year. Some slump.

Tiger has so much pride and determination, and these are intangible commodities that make sure he's always where he needs to be mentally.

When I played Tiger in the final of the Accenture World Match Play in La Costa, I was having breakfast with him and Butch Harmon. I turned to Tiger and said, 'If you chip in or hole a long putt, I don't want you running around punching the air or I'll give you one of these,' showing him a fist. He just said, 'Don't worry, at your weight and physical state you won't catch me anyway.' He was quite right then, but not now.

A lot was also made of the time at the halfway stage of the match when he went straight to the range and I sat on my golf bag smoking a cigar and making calls on my mobile. That was another case of my being totally happy with what I was doing. If I'm comfortable with what I'm doing then I can accept the outcome.

Gary Player once gave me a bunker lesson in Sun City, and afterwards he sent me a letter encouraging me to believe that I would win a major. Whether or not it happens is down to me and a little luck, but you have to believe it's going to happen.

My good friend and ISM stablemate Lee Westwood has so far had the mental edge on me; he was born stronger than I was in that department. We travel together and practise together, and have a friendly rivalry that always seems to help, so hopefully we will drive one another on to claim the game's greatest prizes.

Winning ugly: Making a score when you're below your best

Darren: One of the key aspects that I've worked on with Karl is getting the ball around the course when I am at less than my best. I know that when my manager Chubby Chandler first talked to Karl about working with me he was concerned about the way I would sometimes let a score slip if I wasn't in contention to win. I could easily fall off the radar and tumble down the leaderboard. I now take much more pride in finishing, say, seventh as opposed to tenth. It's not what I would want ideally of course, but I now realise that finishing seventh this week might just be a springboard to a win next week, instead of losing interest this week and letting that slipshod attitude carry forwards for another week and another tournament.

Tiger Woods' performance at the 2004 WGC Matchplay was a perfect example of a golfer who was at odds with his game, but had the mental toughness to grind out a win. Tiger struggled with his driver against Australia's Stephen Leaney in the semi-final, and in the final head-to-head against Davis Love. Time after time he was able to produce remarkable recovery shots and maintain his outstanding ability to hole crucial putts when necessary.

The lesson is simple. Even arguably the greatest player the game has ever known cannot completely rely on or trust his technique all the time; bad shots do happen. What Tiger has is complete trust and faith in himself, and an ability to keep grinding out a score even when he is way below his best.

So, rather than falling into the trap of believing that good technique can protect you from bad shots, learn to accept the fact that the ball will not always behave as you would like. No one, not even Woods, has complete control over the ball, but what you can control is your reaction to where the ball goes.

You need to ask yourself if your normal reaction to poor play works for you. Does getting angry and beating yourself up, questioning your technique, being miserable, actually assist you in producing the best golf that you are capable of? If not, take a leaf out of Tiger's book and learn to 'win ugly'. The opposite of this is what we would call a downward spiral, where your game goes into freefall after a couple of poor shots.

Karl: Generally this is a result of something called 'thought chains' – the way the mind links one thought to another very quickly, usually producing a downward spiral of negativity. This is usually something like, 'There's that hook again;' 'That swing felt terrible;' 'Those lessons aren't working;' 'I'm useless at this game;' 'In fact I'm useless at most things.' And so on etc., etc., until you're trying to find the number of The Samaritans or looking for the nearest tall building or sharp knife.

The trick when this happens is to shout 'Stop!' inside your head, perhaps even see a stop sign in your mind's eye. And commit to keeping your mind open to the possibility that the next shot/swing could indeed be a good one, as opposed to convincing yourself of the lie that it's certain to be a bad one.

Fear is definitely a factor in missing short pressure putts. Without doubt anxiety has an affect on the actual mechanics of the stroke. It has been proven scientifically that when a golfer is confronted by a

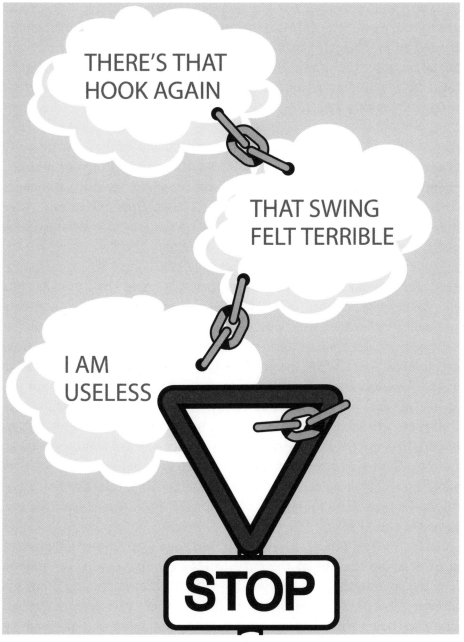

Put a stop to the deadly thought chains.

situation that provokes anxiety, it is imperative that he reduces the amount of technical thinking about the stroke and instead allows himself to be immersed in vivid imagery of the line he wants the ball to travel into the hole. This imagery actually allows the body to respond by going on to autopilot and just reacting to the line that he sees in his mind's eye.

Darren: One of the greatest putters of my generation has undoubtedly been my good friend Davis Love III, yet there is nothing complicated about his style. He looks at the line, takes one practice putt, stands up to the ball, looks at the hole once, and then fires. He doesn't give himself any time at all to allow negative thoughts to enter his head, and consequently reduces the chance of error.

Karl: There is no more important part of the game than putting, but the vital role of the eyes in holing out is often completely misunderstood. When you look at the line of a putt from behind the ball, your eyes are basically taking a snapshot image of that line from ball to hole. Now the key aspect to holing the putt is to keep the image of that line as clear as possible in your mind's eye. The more vivid the image of the line into the hole, the more putts you will sink. Unfortunately many golfers see the line initially, and then start to distort that image. Having too many practice strokes from the side of the ball is one of the worst habits to get into because you are now standing and looking at the hole on a different line, thus distorting the original image. Also, looking at the line from back, front, and side can have the same effect.

After he has picked his line you will see Darren having practice strokes facing the line of the putt, in effect looking down the line he is going to hole the putt on, looking with both eyes directly down his intended line, burning an image in his brain of the route of the ball into the hole. With this image in mind, his body can respond by sending the ball down the line of the image and into the hole.

The physical centre

Most of you will have seen Jonny Wilkinson during the Rugby World Cup going through his strange crouching routine prior to kicking yet another goal. Jonny is actually using a technique taken from baseball. As he goes through his routine, Jonny is taking deep abdominal breaths and placing his attention on his physical centre, a spot a couple of inches below his navel. This is literally the centre of your body, the balance point. With your attention fixed on this centre point, the effect can be a dramatic balancing of body, but also a calming of the mind as those busy head thoughts subside.

So if you are about to challenge for the Open, win your first monthly medal, or break the 100 for the very first time, and you start to notice your mind racing, just set up for your practice swing and place your attention on your centre, breathe deeply, and you will notice a pleasant feeling of balance and control. Keep your attention in your centre as you swing and trust your swing to send the ball towards the target.

It's also important to keep your mind on your own game rather than involve yourself with anything to do with your playing partner, because one of the most damaging and distracting emotions that we can feel on the course is resentment. If you play golf and you are honest you will know exactly what I mean.

You start off with two great shots to the first, well struck, on in two to the par four, while your opponent hits a scratchy tee shot, a sloppy second, not a great third, and then drains the par putt from 25 feet while you manage to take three putts, missing from three feet, and take a bogey. The pattern continues, and increasingly you can hear that little voice inside your head getting louder and louder saying, 'This is not fair, I don't deserve this! What a lucky so-and-so.'

This emotion tends to build and build to the point that it becomes a massive distraction and stops you from focusing on the only thing that you can control, which is you and your own game. You become so obsessed with the good fortune all around you that your concentration

Focus on your centre to quieten the mind and relax the body, just like Jonny Wilkinson.

and state control fly completely out of the window, and another round that you could possibly have salvaged is lost. Your swing didn't cost you the day, but your attitude certainly did.

There are three keys to overcoming resentment. First, remember that you deserve nothing on the golf course. Jack Nicklaus once said that golf was not meant to be fair, and with this in mind you can make a commitment to keep focusing on the only thing that you can actually control which is your reaction to the chaos that is the game of golf.

Secondly, ask yourself what game are you actually playing? Are you playing golf or are you playing the 'what will they think of me' game? And if you're playing that game, recognise that it's a game you will never ever be successful at, because no matter how you perform on the course you cannot force other people to think about you in the way that you would like.

Thirdly, actually think back and run a video in your mind of the last time you reacted badly and found yourself resenting bitterly what was happening on the course. As you bring that to mind, how stupid do you look and how silly was the reaction?

Controlling your emotions

Darren: It may well be that I have been given certain talents with regards to the physical aspects of the game. I feel very grateful that as a result of a lot of hard work and, some would say, a lot of natural talent, I can hit most shots that a golfer would want in his armoury. However there is no doubt that my greatest challenge, as most of you would recognise, is the ability to control my emotions. Karl talks about the 'caveman within', and I would be the first to admit that my particular caveman has on occasion run riot. That said, as I have gained a greater knowledge, over the past couple of years, of how the emotional part of the brain can cause such damage to our golf game, I have definitely improved. By no means am I the finished product, but at least I feel that with the tools and techniques that I now use I am getting closer and closer.

One of the easiest things in golf is to become distracted, but it is also one of the most destructive because a golfer must be fully focused every time he is ready to pull the trigger.

Karl: Over 85 per cent of the time that you're out on the golf course you are not actually playing golf. The quality of what you do and how you use that 85 per cent will have a dramatic impact on your performance in the 15 per cent of the time when you are playing the game.

Control "the Caveman within" or he will control you.

The irony for most golfers is that they have never looked at this non-golf time as being important, nor have ever considered taking some coaching in this area.

A couple of years ago Padraig Harrington made a conscious decision to 'lighten up' in between shots. When you watch Harrington play he is arguably one of the toughest players in the world mentally, and has an unbelievable ability to grind out a decent score when playing badly.

Watch his demeanour closely – he's often smiling and joking, his head is up, his body language good. 'When I smile in between shots,' he has said, 'the lie on the next one often seems better.'

When we laugh or smile our body releases a chemical called serotonin, a feel-good natural drug that actually cools our brain, focuses our mind, and allows us to function at our peak. How often do we say about a player who is great under pressure that he has a 'cool head', whereas someone who 'loses it' is often labelled a 'hothead'. Well, now you know why, and you can decide which route you are going to take in the future. Lighten up and shoot lower!

Is there any game in the world likely to push your buttons in the way that golf does? The big problem is not so much the shot that you have just hit badly, nor even the fact that you have got really angry; it is how long that anger lasts, and how long it stays in your system, and the effect it has on your game over the next few holes.

You often don't pay for anger straightaway, but at some point you will. This isn't a science lesson, but when you get angry the emotional part of your brain is put on full alert. This part of your brain doesn't think, it just reacts. Think of this part of you as the 'caveman' within. When this guy is out of the cave he really wants to do one of two things: run away very quickly, or stand and fight. Now this is a great reaction if you're faced with a growling sabre-toothed tiger, but not so great if you have a little innocent white ball sitting on a piece of green turf with a sliding left-to-right two-foot breaker.

You've heard that good rhythm is important in your swing, and that feel and touch are useful? Well, all of these wonderful attributes go out of the window when Caveman is around. The really big problem is that once he comes out of his cave he will not go straight back in.

Managing anger and the emotional brain is a key mental skill, just as much as reducing your fade is a key physical skill. It may also help in the rest of your life too. We all buy into the idea that we can 'fly into a rage'; well, how about the concept of 'flying into a calm'? The principle is the same – we just need to know how to trigger calm.

NUGGET

Probably the most effective anger management tool I have come across is called the 'clear-the-air breath'. Imagine when you play your shot that, after you have hit it, you are going to walk 10 paces, and at that point you will exhale all the air in your lungs. You literally 'clear the air', and as you do this the shot is over, done, finished. You may wish to do what many of the tour players I work with do, and actually say 'Done'.

To be really angry we have to be breathing in a certain way, high and shallow in the chest. So as you clear the air you clear the way to get the game back on track.

The skill of keeping your head 'while all around are losing theirs' was never better illustrated than by Retief Goosen when he won the US Open and the European Open during 2004. The Goose is the personification of calm, someone who seems completely unflappable but at the same time maintaining a steely inner determination. Calmness breeds confidence, and a move to the next level.

Golf is very different from other sports in that your opponent cannot directly do anything to affect you, whereas in football I can take the ball off you, in tennis I can power my serve past your return, in snooker I can pot you off the table – so confidence in being able to overcome your opponent is obviously paramount. Yet in golf it is down to us and only us, nobody can pick our ball up or block the hole, the real blockage occurs from within. When we have 'calm' we are able to resist and ride out the inevitable chaos that occurs out on the course, we stay stable, we stay able to deal with whatever is thrown at us.

The power of imagery

Darren: I have never been much of a scientist, but I remember Karl saying once that Einstein would have made a great golfer because he always talked about the power of the imagination. I think I'm right in saying that one of Einstein's favourite quotes was, 'Imagination is more important than knowledge because knowledge can only tell us where we have been, whereas imagination points the way to where we may go in the future.' How true that is for golf. We may 'know' what we are doing wrong in our swing, but are we able to change it?

When you think of kids playing golf you can see imagination being allowed to flourish. How often as youngsters did we pretend to be one of our golfing heroes, and then produce magical shots as the body responded to the instructions created by the power of our imagination?

Unfortunately as we get older and supposedly wiser we tend to lose the ability to use our imagination. It could well be said that the more that we know the less we imagine! In particular with golf and technique, the more we become immersed in the details of swing planes, arcs and clubhead delivery angles, the less we are able to conjure up images that can send the ball to its target. Often the way we practise, hitting ball after ball from the same spot, can dull the imagination to the point where it becomes redundant through lack of use.

Use your imagination

When Jack Nicklaus was once asked to piece together an identikit of his perfect golfer, he chose Seve Ballesteros to play all the shots requiring imagination. The Golden Bear also said that it was the greatest quality a golfer could have. I won't argue on that point because some of the best shots I have ever played have been ones that I could see clearly. The more I am unable to see the shot, the less likely I am to hit a good one.

Interestingly, when we think of how Seve developed his game as a boy by just using a three iron, we realise that he would have had to use terrific imagination to conjure up some of the shots he needed to play with just the one club. He is without doubt one of the greatest geniuses ever to play the game, but he 'trained' his imagination as a young boy. Nicklaus also said that he has never played a shot, even in practice, without a vivid image of the trajectory of the ball, and even how it would behave on landing. Jack has been training his imagination for over 40 years.

From my own experience, playing tough links courses as a boy in Northern Ireland forced me to utilise my imagination to combat the challenges provided by the wind and the golfing terrain. So begin to recognise the importance of practising in a way that will 'light up your imagination'. If you just keep hitting balls in the same old way, with the same old routines, unfortunately all you will get is the same old results, only you will experience an ever-growing sense of frustration at the amount of work you are putting in to the game with a distinct lack of reward.

Karl: Practising in a way that involves your imagination, and the use of imagery, is not only vital for your development as a golfer, it's also a lot of fun. Tiger has often talked about the fun that he had in the early years of his development out on the range, working with his father on many different shapes and trajectories of shots. They would literally conjure up new shots to play, big high draw, low soft cut, raking straight low shots, all the time stretching the boundary of Tiger's imagination, and also, as a by-product, giving him an increased feel and awareness of the club face and what he would have to do to exert control over the golf ball.

NUGGET

The game I recommend for you to work on your imagination and shot control is what I call the nine ball drill.

Basically you have   Draw   Straight   Fade
    High
    Neutral
    Low

You just work through the grid seeing if you can hit all of the nine types of shot that are available to you: Low Draw, Neutral Draw and High Draw, and then on to the other shapes. Of course your ability to do this will depend a lot on your skill level, but even if your handicap is quite high you can begin to work on the principle that if you can hit the ball off to the right, and then off to the left, then you will in time be able to find the middle ground which is straight. For the better player it is a wonderful way to practise as it keeps your practice interesting and also makes you aware of the shape of shot that you can really trust out on the course.

Not only can good images allow you to shape the ball, they can also help you to change any technical errors in your swing. This is because the part of your brain that swings the golf club responds to images rather than words. For instance if I am telling myself to 'slow down' in the swing, my brain has very little to work with because how much should I 'slow down', and relative to what?

Fix your tempo through imagination, using the three 'wiper' speeds.

36

On the other hand, a great image that has allowed many players to find a rhythm that they can work with and play effectively from is that of windscreen wipers on a car, and the 3-speed mechanism that they employ. Imagine being in your car when a light drizzle is falling on your windscreen; you flick on the wipers and they move across the screen quite slowly and deliberately. Now imagine making swings at that speed, probably a very controlled shot totally under your control but with less distance than normal. Now imagine the rain is increasing in intensity, and you adjust the wipers to a more regular and consistent speed across your windscreen, just the right speed to allow you to see clearly. By the same measure, the shot that you could see in your mind at this speed would probably be your 'normal' tempo, that just-right speed that has the club under control but is able to send the ball out there.

The rain is now absolutely lashing down, pelting on to the windscreen and forcing you to adjust to top wiper speed. The wipers do their work furiously but still efficiently to keep you safe. This is your full-out swing; this is going for the max, par five, wide open and time to give the ball a ride. Long ball time!

By having these images of the wipers stored in your brain you can go to the range and practise your three 'wiper' speeds and begin to notice how your golf ball and your swing respond to the differing tempo, so that on the course you can 'flick your tempo switch'.

Self-talk:
Be careful what you say –
to yourself

Darren: When we take time to tune into some of the things that we say to ourselves with that little voice we all have in our heads, the results can be amazing. If anybody dared speak to us in the way we speak to ourselves they would be in big trouble. But as I have learned in the last few years, most of what we are saying to ourselves, and the way that we say it, is pretty much unconscious. We don't know that we're doing it because we have done it that way for so long. The first step is to become aware and actually just notice what that voice is saying. As Karl has often said to me, 'You can't change something unless you know what it is!' Once you become aware, you can then do something about it.

Karen Stupples' amazing victory against the odds in the Ladies' 2004 British Open highlighted an often understated and undervalued mindset – resilience.

Karen's story is not one of privilege and inevitable destiny; it is a tale of sheer guts and determination to achieve her dreams and ambitions. Having to make ends meet with jobs like cloakroom attendant and waitress emphasised the fact that she had decided to maintain her dream of finding out just how good she could be at the game of golf. Perhaps most importantly, she said that her victory in the Open wouldn't make her happy, as she was already happy anyway.

Be careful what you listen to on your internal CD player.

NUGGET

Think back to the last time that you had a bad day playing golf, and just imagine if there had been a recording made of all the things that you said to yourself. If anybody else listened to this CD, do you think that they would be able to work out if you were having a bad day?

What would the tone be like? Encouraging, positive, upbeat? What would the dialogue be about? How capable you are, your chances of bouncing back? Where would the voice be coming from? Inside your head, outside, someone else's voice?

The amazing thing is that in most situations we would never speak to anyone else in the way that we speak to ourselves. I always say to the players, 'If you're going to beat yourself up, you need to do it properly.'

To take charge of this internal CD player and start to treat yourself with a little more respect is one of the key strategies for winning at golf and winning at life. It's one of the most important skills that you can develop for yourself, coach in others, and help your children to learn.

Many people absolutely torture themselves with their internal dialogue. Over the next couple of rounds try stepping out of the action and just listen to what's actually going on. Most of this internal dialogue has become so habitual and so unconscious that you're unaware of its presence and effect.

Go out next time and just tune in to what's occurring; you may even start to smile at the abuse and torture that you're inflicting on yourself. After the round, take a pen and jot down a couple of the things that you have said to yourself out on the course. When you actually see this on paper you will see it for what it is – ridiculous.

This first step is vital though, because you can't change something unless you know what it is! Have fun with this and maybe even observe the self-torture your playing partners are inflicting upon themselves.

Martina Navratilova, possibly the greatest women's tennis player of all time, said, 'The moment of victory is so short that you have to enjoy the journey, you have to love the process.' The fact that Navratilova is still playing tennis close to her 50th year is testimony to the fact that she just loves to play the game.

Just a game?

The same can be true of your game too. Have goals, yes, decide that you want to see how good you can be, but always bear in mind that this is a game, and that games are meant to give you pleasure. Not for one minute am I saying that results aren't important, but just realise that having fun and being in the moment are the entry points to you being the best golfer that you can possibly be.

The legendary Michael Jordan summed it up when he said, 'Just let me get on to that basketball court, let me play, because that is when I come alive!'

Karl: So much of the time out on the course we spend inside our own head, listening in on that internal CD player of self-talk. Most of the time what we are tuned into makes anything but pleasant listening. Yet this internal CD player will, and does, have a dramatic impact on how we feel and in turn how we play.

CHAPTER 7

Nervousness?
It's only feelings

Darren: Although Greg Norman was my hero when I started looking at golf as perhaps my future, I have always been aware of the influence Jack Nicklaus has had on the game. Up until the era of Tiger Woods, few golfing pundits would argue that the greatest golfer who has ever played the game is Jack.

The strange thing about Nicklaus's greatness was that it was the sum of the parts rather than individual aspects – apart from one. That special strength which Nicklaus possessed was probably the finest golfing brain ever. Some of Jack's comments over the years give us nuggets of gold in terms of how he thought, and show us ways in which we can take our own game to another level.

It was very interesting to hear Jack say that he felt that he didn't really win Majors; he waited for other people to lose them. He went on to say that on the back nine on Sunday he felt that he would continue to make good decisions when those around him would start to get panicky and make some poor ones.

Jack also made one of his most profound statements when he said, 'Give me that feeling on the back nine of a Major, that's what I hit all the balls in practice for.'

De-label feelings and change the meaning.

Notice though, he didn't say, 'Give me that feeling of nervousness.' Nicklaus had taken the label off the feeling that he had in his body, and reframed the sensation as something to look forward to.

Karl: From this we can learn a very important lesson, that if we notice sensations in our body and put a label of nervousness on to them, we will come to fear that sensation and the situation. If, however, when we change that label and almost welcome the sensations, the irony is that the sensations tend to settle down and we can learn to control the situation. Much of this is due to the conditioning that we receive. From an early age we are taught that the feelings that you get in your body on the first tee are 'first tee nerves'; nobody ever told us that it was 'first tee anticipation'. Just imagine how different things could be if you actually looked forward to and welcomed those feelings.

Notice the feelings in your body when you get in certain positions on the course, but take away the limiting label that you have learnt to put on those feelings. As you notice them, just class them as energy. Then you have the potential that Nicklaus had, to reframe the sensations as something neutral, as opposed to something that you should dread.

The master key:
Correct breathing

Darren: One of the highlights of the 2004 European tour season was the stunning form of my fellow Royal Portrush member Graeme McDowell, who rose from a lowly 90th in the order of merit to a top 10 position, narrowly missing a Ryder Cup place. One of the high spots of the year was Graeme's round of 62 on the Old Course at St Andrews during the Dunhill Links trophy, equalling the course record.

Quite a lot of Graeme's success, according to Karl, is down to the part played by his breathing.

Karl: Graeme pays a great deal of attention to his breathing, particularly when he's putting. His breathing system plays a big role in allowing him to access a state of mind that allows peak performance under extreme pressure.

It would seem strange that something we do automatically each and every day could be such an essential part of a top golfer's armoury. Yet if there is one single skill I would ask you to develop, not only for your golf but also for your whole wellbeing in general, it would be the art of correct breathing under pressure.

Having asked countless people over the years to show me how they would take a deep breath to relax, I would go so far as to say that not more than five per cent of the population have any idea of how to breathe correctly. Because breathing is such an unconscious action, most of us are completely unaware of how we breathe when we get anxious.

The classic mistake people make is to breathe high and shallow in their chest, thus actually increasing the feelings of nervousness.

NUGGET

The fundamentals of correct breathing are:

When you inhale, keep your chest still and allow your belly to expand like a balloon.

When you exhale, keep your chest still and let your belly contract again.

Slow your breath down and let each inhalation and exhalation be of even tempo.

Make your breath silent and smooth.

It's important to understand that every state you go into, be it anger, anxiety, fear or joy, will have a corresponding breathing pattern to it. So to be really nervous we have to be breathing in a certain way, usually high and shallow in the chest. As we have already mentioned with other mental skills, you are probably completely unaware as to how your breathing patterns change as you get a little anxious on the course. Take some time to develop the skill of effective breathing, and be very careful to avoid the mistake of taking this advice lightly because of its apparent simplicity. I would go as far as to say that if you want to improve your golf you need to improve your breathing patterns before each shot that you play. As you develop this skill you will find that the principle applies just as readily in many other areas of your life. In the fast-paced, highly pressurised world we live in, anything that allows us a little more calm and peace of mind has to be worth exploring.

Darren: If there is effective breathing then there is definitely effective practice. Andrew Coltart,a good friend and former Ryder Cup player, admitted recently that he felt he had wasted a good number of years standing on practice grounds all over the world mindlessly hitting balls, working on swing positions and trying to hit the ball dead straight. He felt that his brain had been numbed by just going through the motions in an attempt to fashion the impossible dream of the 'perfect swing'.

Karl: I completely agree in that the mind needs to be involved in practice just as much as the body, and for that to happen the brain constantly requires challenge and novelty. We really do need to move away from the myth of 'muscle memory', and understand that every golf swing begins in the mind not the body. Once the mind is correctly engaged, the body can be allowed to follow and will respond beautifully.

One thing that we know for certain from the world of psychology, as we have already seen, is that the body performs actions better when it is responding to images rather than words. 'Maintain your spine angle' means little or nothing to your body, but the image of a pin running through your neck and spine, and you rotating around it, can produce a completely different golf swing.

Imagination is another key element of bunker play. 'Explosion' and 'blast' are just two of the universally used terms when considering what type of shot to play, but these are words that tend to lead to steep chopping actions more appropriate to excavation than to removing a ball from a bunker. Most pros agree that the divot you take in the sand is key, and a thin shallow is the optimum way to play bunker shots efficiently.

Three images that I use seem to work particularly well in terms of creating a mental picture that produces the correct cutting action. The images are, of all things, meat. The first image is of a big thick Sunday roast, and if you struggle in the traps you are probably removing sand the size of a Sunday roast. Next image, better but still not correct, is that

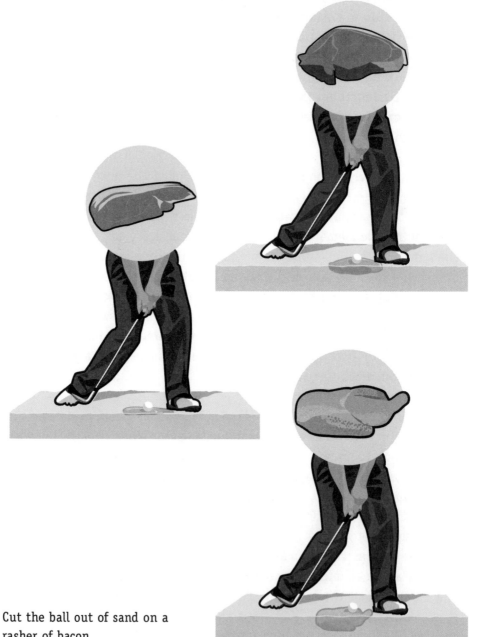

Cut the ball out of sand on a
rasher of bacon.

of a piece of fillet steak. If your bunker play manages to just get the ball out, but often falling woefully short, then you're probably a fillet-steak divot taker. The real key, and the way of the expert, is the bacon slice, a thin but neat cut of meat. If you take divots like a slice of bacon, you will be allowing the club to slide through the sand, and allowing the ball to pop out and ride on this cushion of sand.

The image of the bacon slice held in your mind will change your bunker play by programming your body to take just the right amount of sand.

Stuck over the ball?
Create a 'go' signal

Darren: Many of you will remember when Sergio Garcia got to the point where he could hardly take the club away from the ball. Waggle after waggle, re-grip after re-grip, and Sergio appeared to be getting deeper and deeper into the thick stuff. At one point in a US tournament he was filmed making up to 30 waggles, and I remember once at Sun City when it looked like he would never be able to hit the ball. The whole process became painful to watch as his form took a distinct downturn, and he even had his hands taped to the club at one stage in practice as he searched for a remedy.

The problem the Spaniard had encountered was one familiar to golfers everywhere: he wasn't receiving what Karl refers to as the 'go' signal.

The 'go' signal is that internal sense that everything is OK and we can proceed with the shot at hand. It's the unconscious part of your mind saying, 'Go ahead.'

At the time, Garcia said that he 'just couldn't get comfortable', and so the more he waggled the more he moved away from his 'go' signal.

The problem was solved after he did some work with his father, whereby they agreed on a specific number of waggles as part of the routine. This is the key to overcoming any feelings of being stuck over the ball in the set-up position.

As human beings we need a system or a routine that we can fall back on under pressure. We need a series of steps that take us to our destination. The reason we are taken through a safety procedure on every flight we make is to ensure that we have a set routine to follow should any difficulties arise.

As a golfer you have to decide how many waggles you're going to make, how many times you will look at the hole, how many times you will shuffle your feet, and so on. Whatever it is that you do, develop a system that is the same every time, so that when the heat is on you, the routine will carry you through and allow you to perform to your true potential. We are creatures of habit, and the more we do something the more it embeds itself in our neural pathways in the brain to become a habit. So the more we waggle the club the more we are training ourselves to do even more waggles! Not unlike the person who can't leave the house because he has to keep going back to check that the doors are locked. It's as if the brain's warning system which allows us to proceed with something is working overtime and is too sensitive. Once you have decided on a set number of waggles and then let the swing flow, your brain feels able to 'let go' on a more consistent basis.

For me it's not so much what you do in the routine as the fact that you have a series of steps that build up to a point of action that becomes automatic, just as it is automatic for you when you get in your car to reach for the seat belt and then turn the key in the ignition.

The effects of memory

Darren: I think that one of the biggest challenges we all face on tour, given the amount of downtime we have available to us, is how much a poor round can potentially affect us. Once a round is finished, it's all too easy to go back to the hotel room and play back over and over again the missed putts and poor shots.

One thing I've learnt from Karl in terms of how the mind works is that 'whatever you review, you rehearse'. In a nutshell, when you think about and review a poor shot or a bad swing, as you play the action out in your mind's eye you are actually rehearsing how to do it again. The more you think about it, and the more vivid the memory, the stronger the rehearsal. As I now understand the way you use your memory and its effect, this is something that you need to be very careful with.

Also, the culture on tour tends to be one of 'misery loving company', because it's human nature to focus on the mishaps and disasters. So make a point of avoiding the prophets of doom and the 'Woe is me' brigade, because the more you dwell on your inevitable failures the more you create the opportunity for them to happen all over again.

In his book *How I Play Golf*, Tiger Woods says that the secret to the mental game is the ability to recall good shots instantly, and to let go of failure. This is an excellent piece of advice, but for most of us it runs contrary to the programming that we have received all of our lives.

Success and failure

If you go back to your schooldays and recall what you thought was a great piece of homework, you may remember all the big red crosses when you received your book back from the teacher, highlighting your mistakes. But we never had all the correct sentences underlined!

We're fascinated by reality TV, where most of the shows seek to highlight a person's weakness or inadequacy so that we can vote them off the show or enjoy the moment when Donald Trump or Sir Alan Sugar says, 'You're fired.'

When golfers go for a lesson, generally the first thing they will say to their pro is, 'Tell me what I am doing wrong,' because as a culture we are programmed to focus on our faults.

Yet Tiger tells us that his brain works differently. The attitude to failure that Sir Clive Woodward instilled into the England rugby team before the World Cup win outlines a way of thinking different from the norm.

Woodward said that he changed things around with his players in that when they had been beaten or had played badly, they went for a meal and allowed the bad day to pass before they started to put things right. They didn't react emotionally to a poor day. On the other hand, when they performed magnificently, they stayed behind and discussed how they had played so well, and the next day they were in training early to replay the terrific moves of the previous day. In other words, they focused on what they did right when they played well, and let go of any failures on a bad day.

Karl has shown how this method can be used in golf.

Karl: Working with tournament golfers, I have found that this mindset can transform performance by re-wiring the brain to focus on what you want, as opposed to dwelling on failure.

How can you take action with this in your own game? You need to begin by writing out what I call the 'three-shot diary'. After every round

Take charge of your memories with the 'three-shot' diary.

you play, you should write out in detail the three best shots of that day, including any swing thoughts or images that you had during the shot. By recalling the good shots, you make yourself replay them in your mind, with the result that you literally burn into your neurology the ingredients of success. With every entry into your diary you are, so-to-speak, placing a deposit into your confidence account which you will be able to draw upon at some point in the future.

Taking control of how you feel

Darren: Dr Bob Rotella, the sports psychologist and golf expert, once said to me that the single most amazing part of his work was the fact that he had to help people to enjoy playing golf again. Bob considered it almost incredible that golfers should actually need assistance in enjoying such a wonderful game.

This is a situation with which Karl is not unfamiliar.

Karl: It never ceases to surprise me how many golfers play the game in a state ranging from mild annoyance to potential suicide. What have we done to a game that can make us feel so good, but is causing so many to feel so bad? It is also a fact that very few people play well when they are miserable, in fact very few things in life are done well with a scowl on your face. I can almost hear a number of you saying, 'I understand that concept, but it's the game that's making me miserable because I'm struggling with my shotmaking.'

The problem with this attitude is that if we can only feel good when we're playing well, then unfortunately we will spend a good deal of time feeling bad! Even the greatest players in the world hit a lot of bad shots. With my work in this area over the past number of years I have come to the conclusion that we have to decide to feel good to play good. In effect you make a conscious decision and commitment that you are going to enjoy your golf whatever happens to the ball. The good news about this

Ben Hogan – great technique and also an incredibly strong mind.

Great friends, great rivals – studying the line of the putt with Lee Westwood.

Rising to the Ryder Cup test – a true challenge to the trained brain.

Above The mentally toughest golfer in the world – Tiger Woods.

Below Tiger entering his zone

Above Even when he is unhappy with his swing, Tiger is still very tough to beat.

Above Padraig Harrington - good or bad, always smiling.

Below Justin Rose – potential for the future?

Above The power of self-belief – Ian Poulter

Below Cool, calm, confident and self-assured, Luke Donald is a future star.

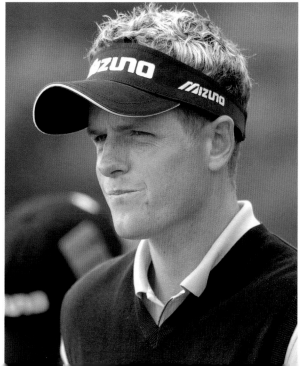

Above V.J. Singh just loves to practise - for him it is anything but hard work.

Right V.J. in full flow – great rhythm is a massive asset.

Right Sergio overcame problems at address with a set routine of a specific number of waggles.

Below Sergio Garcia shows emotion, then is able to refocus.

Left Annika Sorenstam – a product of the Swedish Golf Federation. Mental skills can be taught from a very early age.

Above Playing against the men is Annika's way of pushing her own boundaries.

Left Karen Stupples has triumphed over adversity. Keep chasing your dream.

Below Alison Nicholas. Nice people can be winners.

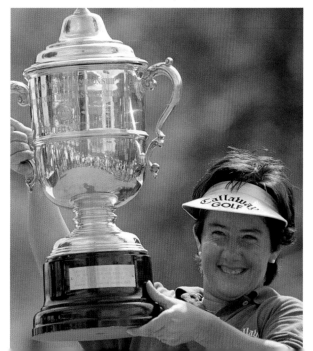

Michael Jordan – the very best. Coming alive on the basketball court, MJ is an inspiration.

commitment is that you have complete control over the outcome. The little white ball may go off line, but it is not in the rules of golf, as far as I am aware, that you have to feel bad about it!

Time and time again I have seen players shake off this attitude and enjoy a completely different experience out on the course.

Again on our theme of the 'frame of mind' that you bring to your game, and its effects, I would just like you to consider what kind of mindset you would take to your next game of golf if it was going to be your very last ever time on the course. This is it, no more games, no more views of the scenery, and no more golfing conversations.

If it were indeed your last game ever, how would you approach the day? What would you be committed to? How much would you be bothered by a missed putt? How much impact would a plugged lie have on you? How would you react to a disturbance on your backswing?

What would it be like if this was your very last game of golf?

The chances are, if it was truly your last round, that most of these minor irritations would then remain just that, and you would probably focus on all the things that you knew you would really miss after you had to stop playing. You would probably truly appreciate the beauty surrounding you. The conversations with your playing partners would take on a special meaning. And the opportunity to play various challenging shots would absorb you. In other words, you would make absolutely the most of whatever the day had to offer.

Now consider your current attitude. Do you play each game with maximum commitment to enjoy the game? Do you deal with the inevitable setbacks along the way? Do you have a sense of perspective?

One thing that is certain for all of us is that at some point we will play our last game of golf. This is fact, we all only have a certain number of games and days on the course left, and not one of us knows when that last game will be. Just imagine if you played golf as though every game was your last? How different would you be? How much would your attitude change?

Well, some day will be your last, so why wait to take on the frame of mind that will allow you to find out just how much pleasure you can get from the game, and at the same time find out how well you can actually perform?'

CHAPTER 12

Finding your own formula for success

Darren: One of the key points that Karl and I want to keep stressing throughout this book is how vitally important it is for you to find out what works for you rather than what may or may not work for someone else. I feel that I'm beginning to know what works well for my own game and, perhaps more importantly, what gets in the way of my playing well. Take advice certainly, find out information, test out different theories by all means, but keep uppermost in mind the idea that what you do with your golf game must fit you and your personality. I have certainly been somewhat guilty of failing to do this in the past, and I'm sure it's something that I will need to be aware of in the future. We all love the idea of a miracle cure, or the elusive 'secret', but over and over again we find out on tour that adhering to certain basic fundamentals and trusting the team of people around us is the key to long-term success.

Vijay Singh is arguably golf's hardest worker, but what he does every day is only what he feels that he needs to do to be at his best. His makeup is such that he wants to step on to the tee knowing he has prepared as completely as he possibly can. This knowledge makes him feel ready to play. He loves to hit practice balls because going on the range isn't real work to him, it's another opportunity to explore what he can do with the golf ball. If you are going on to the range with the flawed mindset that, by hitting balls for hour after hour, day after day, you will have 'paid your dues', and will therefore deserve to play well, then you will be very sorely disappointed.

If Vijay is today's workaholic, then Ben Hogan could be considered as yesterday's. Arguably the greatest ball striker of all time, Hogan was on a never-ending search for golfing perfection. Endless hours on the practice ground 'digging the answers out of the dirt' resulted in a level of consistency that had never been seen before and hasn't been bettered since. Legend has it that Hogan didn't like to play 36 holes in one day around the same course because of the likelihood of him finding his own divot marks in the afternoon round!

The mechanics of Hogan's swing have been dissected endlessly over the past 50 years. The golf world waited with bated breath to hear 'the Hogan secret' which he revealed in Life magazine in the 1950s.

But Hogan must have had an incredibly powerful mental attitude to go with a sound technique. Some of the key thoughts that he later revealed stand the test of time well. He may not have worked with a psychologist but without doubt he had a 'trained brain'. Here are just a few of Hogan's 'mental fundamentals'.

Love the Challenge. 'I have loved playing the game and practising it. Each day made me feel privileged and extremely happy, and I couldn't wait for the sun to come up the next morning so that I could get out on to the course again.

Accept your mistakes. Hogan had a reputation as a perfectionist, but he often stressed that mistakes are human. 'No golfer can always be at the peak of his game,' he said.

Learn from experience. 'I always kept a diary of what I was working on in practice,' he said. 'How else could I be consistent?'

Have single-minded attention. Hogan was famous for his ability to stay focused in spite of what was happening around him. 'Have a very clear intention on each shot,' he said. 'What do you want that golf ball to do?'

Golfing myths:
Be very careful what you believe

Darren: There may be no greater pressure in golf than the first tee of the Ryder Cup, but Karl has an interesting perspective on what pressure actually is.

Karl: A big challenge we face in golf and in life is to become more aware of how we can be hypnotised into believing something to be true to such an extent that we don't question our assumptions, we just go on believing because everybody else believes it!

One of the biggest influences on our beliefs and assumptions is the medium of TV. If it's on TV and an 'expert' has spoken, then it must be true! By just accepting what we hear on TV as the truth we cease to have any choice in our own personal reactions and interpretation.

One of the phrases repeated time and time again on the TV is 'the pressure is building up', or 'he's bound to be feeling the pressure'. What is your definition of that interesting word 'pressure'? What kind of images does it bring to your mind? What exactly is pressure?

I personally have a few definitions of the word. I think that anybody who is serving in the armed forces in a war zone is under pressure. I think a heart surgeon dealing with a cardiac arrest is under pressure. A fireman going into a blazing house is under pressure.

But when it comes to golf are we really under pressure? The problem is that the word 'pressure' will tend to bunch all of those experiences together in our brain so that if we hear that golf is full of pressure, then our physical body will react in much the same way as it would with any other life-threatening situation.

But when we watch our language and start to change the words we use, then our experience can be altered, we don't fall into the collective group hypnosis.

The great basketball legend Charles Barclay had a take on pressure in sport which is about the best I've ever heard in terms of releasing us from the burdensome effects of an overused word. 'Pressure, pressure!' he said. 'Pressure is what I put in my car tyres!' He refused to accept the word as applied to sport, and recognised that whatever happened on the basketball court, his life wasn't in danger.

As we think about our use of words like 'pressure' or 'stress' when applied to so many areas of life, we can begin to see through the illusion and take away the many labels that keep us stuck in terms of our reactions and performance. Let go of these labels and set yourself free to play a game rather than be tricked into believing that you are taking part in a battle.

Darren: Talking of golfing pressure, one of golf's truly magical moments was Paul McGinley's winning Ryder Cup putt at the Belfry in 2002. Faced with a particularly tricky six-footer, McGinley guaranteed his place in Ryder Cup folklore when he summoned incredible reserves of mental strength. By answering the ultimate golfing question of nerve, he ensured that the ball found the bottom of the hole, and the Ryder Cup was once again in the hands of the European team.

I found it fascinating to try and gain an insight into what was going through his mind then, and just how he was able to function in such a situation. It is very interesting that the way he went about holing that putt applies just as much to the club golfer holing the winning club championship putt, or even breaking 100 for the first time.

Pressure is what you put into car tyres!

'At no time did I even consider the mechanics of the stroke,' he said. 'Of course I knew what the putt meant and what it was for, but I became absorbed in the line of the putt. I could see it exactly from beginning to end. My only job at that moment in time was to set the ball off on the line that I had chosen. That was the only thing that I could control'

Basically, Paul simply focused on what he could do as opposed to what might or might not happen if the putt went in. He focused on the task at hand, which was to pick the line of the putt and then set the ball out on that line. His mind was filled with the image of the line of the putt, and so was able to function properly rather than being clogged up with thoughts of technique.

The lesson is that if you want to hole that vital putt, focus your attention on how the ball is going to get to the hole, visualise the line clearly, and then let your body take over and do the rest. Leave the technical work on the stroke for the practice green.

Emotional intelligence on the course: Keeping calm

Darren: Without doubt one of my greatest challenges as a tournament professional is what Karl calls 'emotional intelligence', which for me means in simple terms, keeping my head as opposed to blowing my stack along with a score or a tournament. Keeping cool and level-headed isn't an aspect of my personality that comes naturally. Partly this is down to my intense desire to do well and fulfil my ability. Yet time and time again I have seen what happens when the emotions take over, with others and myself. We have worked really hard on this area, and nowhere was I put to the test more than at the 2005 MCI Heritage, where a big halfway lead should have resulted in a tournament win – but didn't. Looking back over the final two rounds, when my game started to leave me, I can honestly say that I kept to my shot routine, and even thought the disappointment of not winning was great, at no point did I completely lose my cool.

Around the business world 'emotional intelligence' is one of the big buzz phrases, signifying your emotional IQ, or your ability to keep your emotions on an even keel in a pressure situation like closing a sales deal or reaching a crucial decision in the boardroom.

The 'Apprentice' TV series with Sir Alan Sugar has consistently revealed the weakness of certain candidates on an emotional level when under pressure. The ability to think clearly is vital in the world of work, but by the same measure, as we all know only too well, high emotion out on the golf course also equals high scores.

We are not only dealing here with high negative emotion after a bad shot; the up side can be dangerous too. How many golfers begin to think that they're Superman after a couple of pars on the trot, and then make an absolutely stupid decision by going for a shot that's just way out of their capability range? The absolute ideal is to enter the 'neutral zone' where your down is never too down, and your up side is still rational even though you truly enjoy and emotionalise the good shots that you have hit.

Here are five key techniques Karl believes will raise your emotional IQ.

NUGGET

1: Mentally draw a line 10 yards in front of the ball and as you pass this line the previous shot is over, finished, done.
2: Make a commitment to enjoy the time in between shots. It is within the rules to laugh on the course!
3: Always exhale fully after you have hit a shot. Clear the air and clear your mind.
4: Be aware of your tempo, not in the swing but in your walking pace between shots. As a rule of thumb, most golfers get out of their ideal tempo when they hit a few poor or a few great shots. Keep your own pace.
5: Hum in between shots! Yes, crazy as it seems, humming will slow down your active mind and get you back into neutral gear.

Short game:
The money shots

Darren: One part of my game that has come on in leaps and bounds over the past couple of years is my short game. Due to improvements in my technique, alongside a better mental approach and some quality practice, my ability to get up and down in tight situations is light years from where it used to be. It's so easy to go to the practice ground or driving range day after day, and smash ball after ball thinking that your scores will come down. But your ability to shoot low at the highest level of the game is determined by your short game – it's as simple as that. Nobody can hit the ball well enough to cover up a short game weakness.

Pressure also builds on your long game if you struggle around the greens. I know only too well in the past when I felt I had to hit the ball so close to the hole to score well because my touch around the greens was far from world class. In contrast, when you know that you're sharp around the greens, a freedom emerges in the long game as you get a sense that if you do miss a green you know you have the arsenal available to conjure up a recovery.

It has been called the 'zone of contention', the 'money shot', or any of a host of graphic titles, but it basically boils down to this: if you can manage your game from 60 yards in to the flag, if you can chip and putt under pressure, if somehow you can get the ball into the hole when your swing feels dreadful, then you will step up and reach a completely different level of play.

If you can produce the goods in the short game you will be a match for anyone.

How is it that some golfers such as Padraig Harrington can get the ball into the hole in a decent score while not playing too well, while others seem to have to absolutely flush the ball tee to green in order to post a half-decent score? Obviously technique can play a big part in this, but there are some mental strategies from the world's best that could help you turn those three shots into two. Once you have a reasonably sound technique, then the way you run your brain will be the difference between par and bogey.

Karl: Here are my five points to help your short game:

1. Use as often as you can a word which is for me the most important in the English language – possible! Even though you have hit a poor tee shot, your second isn't much better, and you're still 40yds off the green in a non-too-comfortable lie, ask yourself, 'Is it possible that I could get this up and down in two?' The answer to this, no matter how badly you are playing, is of course 'yes, it is possible', and then you begin to create the shot you require in your mind.
2. Eliminate from your language two of the most dangerous words in the English language – 'must' and 'should'. Just say inside your head, 'I must get this up and down to save par', and you may well begin to feel the body tightening and tension increasing as the brain goes on to red alert, as though this was a life-or-death situation. With 'possible' you create a neutral mindset of opportunity. With 'must' and 'should' all you get is stress!
3. With your practice swings, spend much of your time looking at the hole as opposed to thinking about your technique. As you look at the target (just as you would if you were throwing a ball) your brain can begin to formulate a plan and an image of how to get the ball close.

If you are looking down at the ground your focus will shift to technical issues.

4. Always have the attitude that, wherever you place your chip, you will hole the putt after that. If you feel you have to chip the ball absolutely stiff to the hole, you're creating an unrealistic expectation on your short game. Confidence works from the hole backwards.

5. Get really good at holing out from inside 10 feet to support your short game.

As you stand behind the ball deciding on what shot to play, allow your brain to create an image of the entire journey from your club, then the landing spot, and then the ball rolling out and nestling near the flag. This is giving your body a complete description of the task at hand. If you just pick a spot to land the ball on you are only doing half the job.

How do you see yourself as a golfer?

Karl: Golfers are always asking themselves questions about the game, but it's often just as important to ask some questions about yourself. How do you actually see yourself as a golfer? What is your own golfing self-image? Do you walk off the course after a particularly bad day with a feeling in the pit of your stomach that this is just about as bad as it could possibly get? Do you sit down long after the round has finished and ruminate about what disasters befell you out on the course? How do you take a defeat at golf? Does it really hurt inside when you lose, a hurt that can go on for a long time? How do you talk about yourself as a golfer? In the bar after the game, do you take some pride in reminiscing about how lousily you putted that day? Do you suffer a certain sense of inferiority out on the course when you're playing with a much lower handicap player or, in the professional ranks, with someone who has won far more money or tournaments than you? Do you feel that their game is actually more important than yours? Do you then spend a lot of time just making sure you're not getting in the way of their golf, not holding them up in any way, making sure that they can fully concentrate on what they are doing, even if it means rushing your own shots?

So often in the game of golf people tend to lose sight of who and what they really are when playing the game. There is a tendency to base so much of our own self-worth on the handicap or supposed status. It's almost like we create a golfing caste system, where some of us belong and others don't. If we equate too much of who and what we are by the score on a card, or the direction that a golf ball travels, then we put our whole persona under a huge amount of pressure when playing the game.

Did I say 'game'? We feel so good about ourselves on the days when we play well, we want to tell the world how we have done. But on the days when it doesn't go to plan and we play badly, we literally want to hide from the world. We feel terrible inside, and that means we have linked far too much of 'us' as human beings to 'us' as golfers playing a game of golf.

NUGGET

The great Byron Nelson said that he used to dispel much of his nervousness by putting the game into some kind of perspective. He used to reason that whatever happened out on the golf course, he could still go home and his wife would be glad to see him. And even if she wasn't, his dog still loved him. Whatever happened, the sun would still come up in the sky the next day. Byron knew instinctively how to distance himself just enough from the game of golf to allow the right perspective that enabled him to be a great player. This did not mean that he wouldn't try hard in the tournament, and he would have been disappointed if he didn't play well. The fact was, though, that this disappointment didn't stay with him or affect how he felt about himself as a person. He had the supreme ability to really balance his own sense of self-worth with his golfing persona.

You must understand that each and every one of us has a core self, a true self if you like, which doesn't really change. We then have numerous ego states, or other 'parts' of us. These parts are developed to deal with certain situations in the outside world. We probably have a quite different public persona in terms of our work than the one we have with our family. A different aspect of ourselves emerges when we are out with our friends than the one we have when we are with our mother or father.

Perspective – No matter what happens the dog will still love you.

These are all sub-plots in the overall story of our personality. As people, we are actually far more than any one aspect of these varied ego states.

Your golfing personality

So in terms of golf, understand that you need to develop your golfing personality. Be aware that you don't have to be entirely involved with that particular aspect of yourself, so that when you leave the golf course you can prevent yourself at the core level from becoming too affected by the score on your card or the direction that the golf ball has taken. As you become aware of and develop your golfing personality, you can then keep it at a certain distance from your true self. This is a wonderful position to arrive at, and it is one where you can play golf without fear because you haven't invested all of 'you' in the outcome of your game.

The interesting thing about sports is that when you are not afraid to lose, you are also not afraid to win. If I can stand on the tee or green and take whatever happens, I am in a position of freedom, I am truly free because I as a person am not on the line.

I am actually then playing golf again, I am essentially playing a game. It may be a very serious game, I may be playing for the Green Jacket at Augusta, but I am not playing a game that brings into question my whole reason to exist as a human being. I can then go out on to the golf course and give my absolute utmost to the game itself, but I am in no way under the terrible pressure that we impose upon ourselves when so much more than the outcome of the game rests on the score. When you can actually shatter the illusion of the game being the absolute, utmost, important thing, you look at that illusion in a completely new way. Thus you re-create the illusion and can now play the game for all you are worth, with all of your heart.

Karl: It's a bit like becoming really involved in a good game of Monopoly. Once you become so absorbed by the game, you really, really don't want to land on Park Lane if that's where your opponent has one of their hotels. You moan and groan as you lose some Monopoly money, and then feel elated when you are able to win some back. But overall, at a deeper level, you know you're only playing a game. Even though you are not actually playing for your own money, you have created the illusion that you are. This is what makes the game so much fun.

Far too many people are playing golf with such intensity that, if it were Monopoly, they would give themselves a heart attack. The internal pressures they have put themselves under are due to the lack of perspective.

Again, the implication is not to say that results don't matter, because they do. This book is all about showing you how to get the results you desire. Life is all about results. Simply ask yourself to take a new view, with a new perspective of how you go about attaining the results that you truly want. Think about how you're going to feel along the way in the pursuit of those results. If the journey towards the destination isn't fun, if it doesn't give you a sense of pleasure and satisfaction, then you will find that even if you do arrive at your chosen destination (which is unlikely), it has left you feeling somewhat flat and empty.

CHAPTER

17

State control:
Pressing the confidence
buttons

Darren: I can vividly recall the feelings that I had all week at Akron, Ohio, when I managed to win my second World Golf Championship event in 2003. All through the week I had a tremendous sense of calm confidence. I felt good in myself and with my game. On a number of occasions I could easily have thrown the tournament away when put to the test. But without doubt, when you have the feelings of confidence that I enjoyed that week, you can be a pretty tough guy to beat.

The confidence I am talking about is not a swaggering, brash confidence where you are really trying to convince others of how good you are; it's an inner sense or a faith in your ability.

Confidence is a strange thing. It can arrive and disappear all too quickly, yet without it we have little chance of achieving our goals. I am indebted to Karl for giving me a much greater understanding of how confidence is created and, more importantly, how it can be retained.

Karl: 'Calm', 'confident', 'focused', 'in control', are just a few descriptions of how champion golfers describe peak moments of golfing experience. Just imagine what it would be like if you had more control over your state when you play. What would it be like if you decided how you were going to feel, instead of the golf ball deciding it for you?

Champion golfers, indeed effective golfers at any level, take personal control of how they feel. They don't wait for outside factors to make them feel good.

Most people do rely on the influence of outside factors. They have to see the ball flying well, or they have to be scoring low in order to feel good. The problem is that if you wait for outside factors to make you feel confident, then you have very little control. The fact of the matter is that nobody who plays golf can totally control the golf ball, not even Tiger Woods (although he does get awfully close a lot of the time). So if you wait for the ball to make you feel good, you're going to be in for a very rocky and unstable ride. Not to mention the fact that your golf too will be anything but consistent.

What we are about to outline is the information that will put you into a totally new position in terms of controlling your state. This doesn't mean that you will never hit any bad shots, or that you won't get angry out on the golf course. What it does mean, though, is that over a period of time you will start to take more control over yourself. And don't you think this could be very worthwhile to your game?

A feeling of confidence

Confidence! What a wonderful feeling it is when you have the belief that you can achieve anything. The feeling that your swing will send the ball down the middle of the fairway or into the back of the hole. We have heard it said so many times that if only so-and-so had more confidence he would be world class. Or perhaps you can connect with this: If I felt that confident, I would win every time.

What is this thing called confidence? Is it something that comes down from the skies? Is it in some way rationed, something we are only allowed to have now and again?

Of course it isn't like that, confidence is a process. We have to go through a certain internal procedure to make ourselves confident, or for that matter to make ourselves scared. So if confidence is a procedure that we carry out on ourselves, this gives us the opportunity to influence the situation.

If you just wait for confidence to come along as a result of outside influence, i.e. when you're winning or hitting the ball well, then you will spend a lot of time waiting, and your confidence will be as random as the flight of the ball. Have you ever noticed that when you trust your ability, the ball seems to fly straighter? Can you see the paradox? The ball needs to fly straight to make us confident, yet we need confidence to make the ball fly straight! The way we normally go about trying to create this 'false confidence' is by labouring under the ultimate illusion that the past will equal the future, in a golfing sense.

By way of an explanation of this, can you remember a time when you hit balls on the practice range before you played a round of golf, and the ball just flew perfectly? You were right on song, you felt tremendous, your swing was as smooth as silk, you felt really confident that today was going to be a big day. Then you got out on to the course expecting so much, you hit the first couple of drives well, and then it all fell apart. Of course you know the rest of the story, the game went from bad to worse. The 'confidence' that you had out on the range just seemed to disappear into the atmosphere.

On another occasion, you may recall going to the course feeling dreadful, with little or no expectations for the day. You basically just wanted to get round in one piece. You hit the first tee shot okay, made a couple of scrappy pars, and then hit a few shots that felt pretty good. Then all of a sudden the rhythm in the swing returned and you posted a great score, seemingly out of nowhere.

In the seminars, workshops, and personal work we do with golfers, this is an almost universal experience. Can you see what's going on? We continue to hold the illusion that the past should equal the future.

Ultimate confidence at golf starts to arrive when we recognise that what happens out on the course on any given day is open to so many different factors that we cannot control. But what we can control is our reaction to those chaotic experiences out there. When there is a sense of being able to deal with whatever the day throws at us, even if that means our own really bad play, a deeper, more lasting sense of confidence starts to emerge. A quiet, personal confidence can grow which is not dependent on factors we have no control over. It also puts us into a position where we can go out to play golf with little or no expectations. A very wise man once said, 'If you have no expectations, you will never be disappointed.'

The amazing aspect to this mindset is that it provides the foundation and opportunity for a peak experience. Generally, people leave themselves victim to outside occurrences and allow these to dictate how they will then feel. This is often the case with stress. People talk about stress as though it is something we catch, like a virus, yet stressing is a process.

Operating your own software

To feel stressed, you have to do certain things internally and externally. Few people are aware of the fact that stress is an internal procedure which we can actually take a measure of control over. Unfortunately, in our western culture of compensation and blame, the many mediums of information feed us with the idea that the way we feel is the fault of somebody else. Terrible things do happen out there, and there are awful people, but what we need to claim back is our personal ownership of our reactions to what happens in the external world. This knowledge that your state is an internal process then allows you to put yourself in a position to influence how you feel and react to the world.

Confidence works in exactly the same way, and you can either wait for it or you can take charge. It is certainly true to say that when our confidence levels run high our performance takes a great leap forward towards the fulfilment of our potential.

If you think of confidence now, or think of somebody that you associate confidence with, how does it look? How does it feel? What sort of things do we say to ourselves? How do we walk? How are we actually being?

Now, think about and consider your models of confidence, because confidence is a state of mind and a state of being.

Our internal representations and our physiology are the two main roads that lead us into 'being' during any particular state. You influence your states all the time, and up until now it has been pretty random. No one has ever shown you how to change your state. In effect, your states have been controlling you – rather than you controlling your state. Knowing this is key to getting the results that you are capable of. These two main roads are so strongly linked that if you influence one, the other is automatically affected.

Consider two of the truly great players of the game, Ben Hogan and Jack Nicklaus. In these players we see supreme examples of athletes controlling their state. Think about the look in Jack's eyes as he played the back nine at Augusta in 1986, winning his sixth Green Jacket at an age when you aren't supposed to win Green Jackets. How well do you suppose Jack was controlling his state then? Nicklaus knew he could control his state when other people around him were losing their own control.

Hogan took state control to the ultimate degree. He placed himself inside an internal cocoon at the beginning of the round, and didn't emerge from it until the round was over. All the time out on the course he was totally oblivious to what was happening in areas peripheral to his own game. We don't recommend Hogan's solitary approach, but mention it as a supreme example of what is actually possible when we take control of our own brain, not allowing outside influence to knock us off our course.

Physiology and body language

Your physiology is basically the way that your body moves through the world: your breathing, your body language, your posture, the way you walk. Just try this – allow your head to droop down so that it's almost touching your chin, hunch your shoulders over, take a few quick shallow breaths, and tighten the muscles in your hands. Then try to say to yourself, in a whining tone of voice, 'I feel really confident'.

It doesn't work, does it? If your body is moving in a certain way, it will give you a certain feeling. If you wanted to be really down and depressed, then you would have to move your body into a certain posture, and breathe in a certain way, or you would find it a little more difficult to hold on to that state of depression.

How many times have you hit a bad shot, replayed it back in your mind a couple of times, and then trudged down the fairway, looking down at the ground, shoulders hunched? You then wonder why you have suddenly got into a run of dropping shots. For most golfers the fact that one bad shot is hit isn't the problem, but that one bad shot causes a cascade of other bad shots. Just as some people suffer a single negative event that causes them to descend into a pit of despair that can last for days. This bad shot in golf influences the state, and then you compound the state with your physiology.

Take in the image of Tiger Woods striding down the fairway. He looks absolutely magnificent with his head held high, moving freely, breathing comfortably. Compare that image with your own body language when you are playing. When people say that golf is all in the mind, they are in fact a good way out of line. It would be more correct to say it is in the mind and body in very specific ways, as you are now discovering.

As you bring up images of great athletes in any sport, such as Michael Jordan, Muhammad Ali, or Pele, do you conjure up examples of body language that oozes confidence? We have discovered that early in their careers these great athletes made a conscious decision to act confident, even before they had the results to prove it. When you act confident for long enough, you become confident. It really comes down to the question, do you want to wait for success and hope, or do you want to take charge and grab it with both hands?

This is a very profound concept: if you make a conscious decision to walk, breathe and move with confidence, then you will be confident. This is not about becoming a braggart, but it is about a quiet internal appreciation of how each and every one of us can influence the way we feel about ourselves. We were never taught this in school. Most of the time we were just put in our place and made very aware of our limitations. We were conditioned to be, and to feel, very ordinary, and were always being told not to show off. But now you are systematically building your own strong sense of personal resources. You are saying that you have had enough of ordinary results and things are going to be different now.

The other vital component to confidence is your internal representations – the pictures, sounds and feelings that you generate inside your head. Think of it this way, that every time you play a game of golf you have a DVD recorder which is systematically recording all your golfing experiences for you to play back to yourself at any given moment. Now just imagine you ran back the recording of a movie of 'my most embarrassing golfing experience'. Very quickly, as you began to watch this movie again, you would begin to re-experience some of those feelings of embarrassment. So the old movie will have changed your state and created an unwanted new state. It's as simple as that; if you run old movies you will get old feelings, good or bad! The culture of golf tends to keep us playing the horror movies as we constantly focus on our mistakes and errors.

There is a huge difference between being aware of the movies as opposed to reacting to them. Most people are playing horror movies inside their mind, completely unaware of why they feel so bad! Yet when you become aware of your internal movies you can do something wonderful and simple: you can change them.'

NUGGET

Behind every emotion that you feel is a movie. Something is playing on the screen of your mind to make you feel happy, sad, nervous or whatever.

When you change your movie you change how you feel.

Mental fitness:
Training in the mental gym

Darren: When I look back to my early years out on tour, the word 'psychology' was only ever whispered in hushed tones, and nobody freely admitted to working with a 'mind coach'. I am convinced that this is in part due to our lack of understanding about the subject, and to the fact that it's sometimes difficult to pin down what it is. It's easy to see a backswing that's out of plane, or a torso that's lacking in flexibility, but issues like self-belief and focus are pretty difficult to grasp.

How times are changing, though, because in today's modern game if you are not working with someone on your mental game you are without a shadow of a doubt in danger of being seriously left behind. I now understand much more clearly that the mental game has to be worked on in just the same way as your technique or your fitness. What Karl continues to do so well is to simplify what can be a complex subject and make it practical and applicable to the real world.

Most amateur and some professional golfers have an understanding of the importance of the mental side of the game but do nothing about it, because they don't know how to do anything about it or whom to see. They may buy one of those programmes that promise you miracles if you sit under a tree and go into hypnosis, imagining you are Tiger Woods, or telling yourself that you are 'the greatest', or trusting your subconscious powers. That nonsense doesn't work.

Training your golf brain is based on the real world, a world that involves those feelings of stupidity after you have topped the ball off the first tee, or being mad as hell after you have just blown another score, and having that self-doubt constantly knocking at the entrance to the doorway of your mind. It's about becoming the best that you can be by understanding and taming some of your own mental demons and overcoming your self-imposed limitations.

What do you trust?

Karl: To overcome our limitations and to stretch ourselves to a place that we didn't really think was possible is truly a wonderful feeling, and at its heart lies our very nature as human beings.

Why would we need to use psychology in golf anyway? Surely if our swing is good enough, technically sound and solid, then it won't ever break down even under the pressures of competition. If only this were true! How many times have we been on the practice range, hitting the ball beautifully, having just received the green light from our coach – surely today when we get out on to the course we're going to shoot the lights out and finally play to our true potential. Not the case. When you understand the following description of what we have identified as the 'Four Golfing Types' then you will be in a completely different position with regard to your game and you can then start to take action accordingly.

The Four Golfing Types

1. Untrained swing/untrained brain

This golfer is primarily, but not always, the beginner golfer. He is the player who has no technical ability with regard to his swing, no basics or fundamentals, and no conceptual understanding of what a good golf swing is like. He is also mentally untrained with regard to his golf. If you put him out on the golf course he would feel extremely vulnerable, and whatever small amount of golfing ability he had would just crumble.

2. Trained swing/untrained brain

This is the golfer that as a sports psychologist I see becoming more and more the norm. He has worked on his swing, he has taken a bunch of lessons, looks technically sound and hits the ball great on the range and in non-pressure situations. But, when he really wants to play well, when the pressure notch is turned up a little, that wonderful practice-ground swing seems to fall apart.

This golfer has a trained swing but an untrained brain. No matter how many ball he hits in practice, no matter how good he looks on video, he will not fulfil his potential until he deals with the thinking part of his golf.

3. Untrained swing/trained brain

This is the golfer we have all met, the ultimate frustrating player. He swings the club in what has to be described as an awful unorthodox manner, he looks terrible, but he just seems to keep finding the fairway with his funny little shots; he hits some greens, and keeps knocking those putts in. You feel you should beat him, yet he always seems to come through, especially in a tight situation. This player has not got a good swing, but he does have a trained brain, he has the capacity to get the absolute best out of himself and his abilities. He may even hit the ball badly in practice, but get him on to the course and he will play. However, the technical deficiencies in his swing will only allow him to go so far.

4. Trained swing/trained brain

The ultimate player, not only does he swing the club well, but he can also deal with his emotions on the course. Tiger Woods and Annika Sorenstam would be good examples of this kind of golfer. Such players will become the very best that they can be because they have trained both the mental and the physical sides. This doesn't just apply at the top level; whatever standard of golf we are at we can look to train both our golfing bodies and our golfing brains.

Because of the design of the golfer, golf is a game of misses, and the player with the best misses wins.

We are looking here with fresh eyes at the whole area of mental training at golf in the sense of providing you, the player, with a 'toolkit' of coping strategies before problems arise, as well as complementing the skills that have already been put into place. You should have the understanding that mental skills can be developed and improved upon, and that they are part and parcel of training, as opposed to being something to consider if you feel your game is in trouble.

Effective mental training provides you with that inner confidence and outward presence that is the hallmark of peak performance. The effective use of a structured mental skills programme is graphically illustrated by a quote from Niclas Fasth after he finished second in the British Open at Royal Lytham in 2001 as a relative unknown.

'We all got taught how to control our mind by the Swedish Golf Federation,' he said. 'We've got a very good system of bringing young talent through. It is really up to yourself to use it and practise it, but we're taught certain techniques in the classroom and on the golf course from a young age. I don't get too nervous. A couple of times it was difficult, but I really like these situations and you have to have the capability to control your nerves. The most common way is through breathing techniques, it's fairly basic.'

I believe that training your golf brain is divided into four separate but interlinked quadrants: what you do Before the game, During the game, In-between (the time on the golf course when you are not actually playing golf), and After (how your brain processes the experience that you have just had on the course and the profound effect that it can have on future performance).

In many ways, mental training offers you the greatest potential for improvement at golf, but it is the most challenging method because you can't directly see or feel the changes you are making. When you improve the mechanics of your swing, you can see the changes on a videotape. When you train your body, you are obviously able to notice the changes in the way that you look and feel. But mental training is different in that you need to make a commitment to stick with it, and to recognise that the results may not be initially obvious.

Success with the mental game almost sneaks up on you. You start to find that you are holing a few more important putts. You feel a bit better on the first tee. You manage to hold on to your score after a good start. You start to shoot lower. Then you suddenly realise that you are actually a different player.

We live in what I call the 'microwave society'. We want instant change, instant results, just like putting a frozen packet of food in a microwave and then 10 minutes later it's ready to eat.

Golf doesn't work that way, and for the most part neither does life. There are a few lottery winners, but not many. The amazing thing is, though, that when we commit to something and pursue it with our full attention, we begin actually to appreciate the process of becoming as good as we can be. We enjoy the journey, not just the destination.

Not just good on the range

The 'before' aspect of training your golf brain is about two critical components of great golf. First, the state you are in, which means the state of mind and body that you bring with you to the first tee and effective practice. Are you going to continue to practise in such a way that you play wonderful golf on the range? Or are you going to practice in such a way as to become the best player that you can possibly be?

NUGGET

A group of medical students were given lectures in a specially designed classroom. The room was set out so as to achieve maximum relaxation: the lighting was soft, the colours on the walls were in shades that encouraged calmness, the seating was extremely comfortable, and they even had relaxing classical music playing in the background.

Then halfway through the course the group split into two for tests. Group one took their tests in the original 'relaxed' room, while group two took theirs in a new room. This room was the complete opposite: lighting was harsh fluorescents, seating was very uncomfortable, and the walls were painted in drab unwelcoming colours.

The results of the test were staggering.

Group One in the relaxed room had an average grade of 85 per cent. Group Two in the harsh room returned results of 29 per cent.

Is this not similar to our experience at golf? We play great golf on the range and then something happens on the way to the first tee. We get on the golf course and start hitting the ball all over the place, and we assume that our swing has changed. Well, the good news is that the swing hasn't changed. However, your state has altered significantly. On the range you were in a nice relaxed state, but by the time you got to the first tee you were tense.

We need to create a relaxed environment to learn our mechanics, and then we must know how to return to that state on the golf course. Otherwise we will be in this never-ending loop of insanity whereby we hit the ball well in one environment (the range), then go to another environment (the course) where we hit the ball badly, and then go back to the first environment to try to fix the problem.

People who can control their states will to a large extent be able to control their world, and the results they achieve within that world. Most people are totally at the mercy of their ever-changing states because they don't have the faintest idea of how to control the way they feel. The state they are in is usually determined by what's happening in the outside world. If it's a nice sunny day they feel good; if the golf ball is behaving itself they feel confident; if the person they are playing with is to their liking they feel happy. The way they feel is controlled by events that are external to them, and that's not good.

Unfortunately we cannot control external events like the weather, or whom we are playing with, or the state of the course, and if the way we feel is dependent on these conditions then we are in a very vulnerable position indeed. Many of the events in the world we have little or no control over, but what we do have the opportunity to control is our reaction to external events. The ability to be in the right state at the right time for the task or experience at hand is the fundamental difference between those who achieve their goals and live fulfilled lives, and those who don't.

It is first of all vitally important to understand two key issues. First, how do we create our states of mind? We do have the opportunity to control our states, and for golf the state to aim for is what is known as 'Ideal Performance State' (IPS). Second, how do we get into a state?

We go in and out of various states of mind all day long. This can vary from a relaxed state, a learning state, an angry state, a frustrated state and so on. You can already begin to consider some of the states you would like to play golf in.

Movies of the mind

The state of mind that we have is dependent on two key issues, as we discussed in the previous chapter: our internal representations, and our physiology. An internal representation is basically an image which is passing through the screen of our mind. This image may not necessarily be just a picture; it could be a sound, a taste, a smell, or a feeling. Imagine your mind is like the screen of a movie theatre, and the movies are always playing something. This screen never really shuts down. Even when we are asleep it doesn't go totally blank, as we know from the fact that we can remember certain aspects of our dreams.

When we watch a good movie, emotions are aroused within us, such as sadness when we watch Titanic, or excitement with a Bond film. In the same way, our own movies will cause us to feel certain emotions, and thus directly affect our state. The amazing thing is that almost nobody consciously realises the effect of these internal films, and if they do, even fewer people actually take control of what goes on the screen. For most people the internal movies keep on running and running, playing out the same old stuff over and over again at the unconscious level, and producing the same old results.

Up until now you have been stuck in a seat in the movie theatre and someone else is probably running the projector at the back of the theatre so that they can decide whether to make you feel good or bad. What you are going to do now is develop the skill whereby you decide what is going on the screen so that you can reclaim control of how you feel.

This simple exercise will give you a basic understanding of how the internal theatre operates.

Exercise 1

Close your eyes.
Pay attention to your breathing.
Now imagine a golf ball.
Imagine the sound of the ball and club as they meet each other.
Now imagine the feeling of the grip on your driver.

I am sure most of you managed that exercise quite comfortably. You were literally able to put up the sights and sounds suggested to you on the movie screen of your mind. The key point here is: Who controlled that experience? Who had the final say in terms of what went on to the screen? I may well have suggested things, but the ultimate control was down to YOU!

This gives you the experience, possibly for the first time, of taking control of what goes on in the internal movie theatre of your mind. We can make the analogy with a computer where, if you know how to press the right buttons, you can call up a certain program from the software. We could say that our mind is the software of our computer, and our brain is the hard drive.

Now follow up with this exercise.

Exercise 2

Close your eyes.
Pay attention to your breathing.
Think back to a time recently when you played your very worst golf.
What do you notice about the pictures?
What sounds do you hear?

How are you feeling?

Really get into the experience.

Notice how it feels to re-enact vividly the sights and sounds of a really bad day.

Now clear the screen of the mind by thinking about a square box, put a circle in the middle of the box and put a cross through it.

Exercise 3

Now think back to a time recently when you played great golf.

What do you notice about the pictures?

What do you notice about the sounds?

How are you feeling this time?

Really get back into the experience and notice how you feel.

This exercise usually leads to a very important understanding. When you replay the bad event vividly in multi-sensory images in your mind, you usually feel bad, and then you go into something of a negative state and feel quite unresourceful. Yet when you play the good event back in multi-sensory images you start to get good feelings, change state, and feel positive.

It may seem obvious, but most people get into the habit early in their lives of constantly replaying the 'bad movies', not only in golf but in their lives in general. But you now know that you can actually take charge of this process, and that playing the horror movies over and over again has no purpose whatsoever in being a good golfer.

Successful people take the learning from a negative experience and then let go of it. They dwell on the things they do well, and they replay them over and over in the theatre of their mind, thus creating neural pathways that allow them to re-create excellence. A story about Jack Nicklaus illustrates this perfectly.

Constructive forgetfulness

Jack was giving a presentation to a group of eager and attentive golfers at a university attended by one of his sons. During the speech Jack made the comment that he had 'never three-putted on the back nine of a major championship, or missed from inside of three feet'. As Jack opened the floor to take questions, a man put up his hand and said: 'Jack, you say that you've never missed from inside of three feet in a major, but I was watching you last year in the US Seniors Open and that's exactly what you did.'

Jack looked at the man with those piercing blue eyes, and repeated that he had never missed from inside of three feet on the back nine of a major. 'But Mr Nicklaus,' the man insisted, 'I saw it, I have it on film, I can send it to you if you like.'

'No need,' Jack replied. 'I have never missed from inside of three feet in a major, any more questions?'

Now, has Jack Nicklaus ever missed from inside of three feet in a major? Of course he has! Does he remember it? Not a chance, and do you think he cares that he can't remember? Some people would probably say that this is deluded thinking, it's not reality. Well, we all create our own reality, and I for one would much rather be part of Jack Nicklaus's reality in terms of golf than almost anyone else's.

Ask Jack about some of his triumphs in the game and he will be able to give you a chapter and verse account of the minute detail regarding past glories. That is how his brain stores golfing memory. He puts huge emotion into the things that he does well, and for the things that don't work out he takes out the learning experience, attaches no emotion whatsoever, and moves on.

Jack Nicklaus's ability to control his state out on a golf course is legendary, but do you think his ability to do that was influenced in any way by what he chose to let pass through the theatre of his mind? If we could look inside Jack's head and glimpse his internal representations, do you think they would support what he was trying to achieve? The critical element to this is that his ability to focus on what he did right, and let go of what he did wrong after he extracted the necessary learning, is a skill that you can develop, it's not something that is hard-wired into our genes.

All through our early years we are primarily instructed to pay attention to whatever is incorrect (the red marks in your exercise books at school). This has some value in learning subjects like maths and English, but it has no constructive value in sport. This is not saying for one moment that we should deny our weaknesses or our faults; what we are talking about is developing belief and mental toughness, and this does not come from dwelling on our inadequacies.

Our internal representations are not always concerned with the past. We can just as easily play images of what may or may not occur in the future on the screen of our mind. Again, this can have a tremendous impact on the state we encounter in the present moment, certainly before we go out to play.

It becomes almost second nature for many people (at the unconscious level) to be playing out images of impending disaster for upcoming events, be they golfing or otherwise. The only way that a player can get really anxious before an event is by watching movies in the theatre of the mind that have particularly unsuccessful results. Often a player will see himself playing a particular hole badly, then maybe imagine what people may say when he has finished, then remember a previous occasion when he felt very nervous. As he keeps doing all this, without any real conscious awareness, he may then wonder why there is a spreading sense of impending doom about the upcoming event. That isn't good state control. We do actually have some choice in terms of the direction we choose to send our mind. Knowing this can create a very empowered golfer.

Now try this exercise.

Exercise 4

Close your eyes; pay attention to your breathing; imagine standing on the first tee of an upcoming event; notice all of the sights going on around you; hear the starter calling your name on to the tee; be aware of how tight the grip on the club feels and how your stomach is churning; now hit the shot badly; notice the deafening silence around you as the ball dribbles off the tee. How do you feel? Not good, I imagine.

Again a simple exercise, but doesn't it bring into conscious awareness the very thing that you may be doing to yourself before an event? Is it any wonder that you feel pretty anxious about the prospect of the upcoming event?

It does seem almost ridiculous that our mind would want to work against us in this way, but brains just tend to go in certain directions, and after they have gone in one direction a number of times they just keep on doing that, even though there is no benefit whatsoever to the individual.

Again it seems almost part of our culture to preview upcoming events in a very negative fashion. In some situations this may be of some benefit as we seek to consider all the things that may go wrong in the future. When buying a house, for instance, we may need to look at all the potential downsides before we decide, but in golf this mental habit does not really have any place in the pursuit of peak performance. It is a habit of mind, and since a habit is a learnt behaviour we do have the opportunity to change that habit.

Now do this exercise.

Exercise 5

Keep eyes closed and pay attention to breathing. Now think of an upcoming event. Notice that as you step on to the tee, your body feels relaxed and your mind sharp and focused. As you take a practice swing, the flow of motion seems just right; in your mind's eye you can imagine the exact spot on the fairway where you intend to send the ball. Set up to the ball and take one last glance at the target, and as you do this you get that signal to 'go'. Notice the sound of club meeting ball, the feeling of perfect balance as you sense the ground beneath your feet, the sight of the ball sailing into the distance, the ripple of sound around you as people say 'good shot' or 'good swing', and the feeling as you put the club in the bag and start to stride purposely down the fairway.

How do you feel now? Is that not a complete contrast to the previous exercises? Does this not hammer home the message of how powerful the images can be which we allow on our mental screen in the way they affect our feelings, confidence and self-belief?

The second component to our state is our physiology, the way that we breathe, the way that we move, the way that we carry our bodies. This all has a direct bearing on our state.

If you ever get to see the great American motivator Anthony Robbins, who has worked with Andre Agassi among other elite athletes, you will not be allowed to stay slumped in your seat for any length of time if you are a member of his audience. Robbins will have you up stretching, moving your arms, and shaking hands with the person next to you, because he knows that a slumped or cramped body position (poor physiology) will lead you into a poor state, and a poor state will not allow you to take in and learn what he is presenting to you. Robbins is an absolute master at influencing and changing people's states. The way he does this is by changing a person's physiology.

If we think of some of the great golfing champions over the years, Severiano Ballesteros, Nick Faldo, Jack Nicklaus and today Tiger Woods, don't these players move in a certain way? Doesn't their body language create a certain aura? I can vividly remember as a child seeing a then young Ballesteros step on to the second tee in practice at Royal Birkdale in 1983. It was the first time I had seen him in person, and as he walked through from the first tee it seemed this man was about eight foot tall, and carried with him an aura that you couldn't help being affected by. Today Tiger has that same air about him, and he carries himself so magnificently.

From the world of cricket, the greatest spin bowler possibly of all time, Shane Warne, has gone on record as saying that one of the most important things he learnt from the Australian Institute of Sport was the importance of taking charge of his body language, even when the game was going away from him and the day was a tough one.

If you ever have the misfortune to deal with someone who is having a panic attack, you will notice how erratic their breathing patterns are, high up in the chest. The quickest way you can get them back to some kind of neutral state is by altering their breathing to low in the abdomen. Altering physiology causes a corresponding alteration in state.

So to change your state, change your physiology. How can we apply this to our game? So many golfers are in poor states when they're playing because of the way they carry themselves, particularly after a bad shot. The following exercises will coach you on the importance of body language and physiology and how to take control for yourself of the way you feel.

Exercise 6

Describe and write down in detail how a champion golfer moves as he walks on to the first tee. Now write down a description of how he walks in between shots. Then write down what we would see if we were watching a video of you in a similar circumstance, and what we would see in the video after you had just hit a bad shot.

This will provide you with what is known as a contrastive analysis. The first part of the exercise gives you the opportunity to pick out at an unconscious level the elements of body language that you deem most important. The second gives a vivid image of how your own body language is a poor relation to the movements of the champion.

Now I want you to imagine that you are on the course and ready to go to the first tee. Go to the first tee and imagine that you are acting as if you are moving on to the tee like the champion you described. Just notice how different it feels to try on this new behaviour, notice how your body language is different, how you are carrying yourself, how you are breathing, how you look around. Just notice how this feels.

Now do the same down the fairway after hitting a shot. Maybe you hit a bad shot, but instead of your normal slumping walk, looking down at the ground, you carry yourself very differently. How does that feel? What you have done in effect is mentally to rehearse a new way of being on the golf course, so that the next time you play you can become your images as you take charge of your body language and the way that you feel. Body language matters.

Nervousness is a state that you create

For an awful lot of golfers, performance anxiety and first tee nerves are major issues, but most people have little or no idea of how to do anything about these major obstacles to peak performance. If we recognise that nervousness is a state, and if we remember the formula that our state is created by our internal representations and our physiology, then we can actually do something about it.

Take in this statement: 'It is next to impossible to be nervous and to be breathing correctly.' If we are breathing correctly, then our physiology does not support the state of nervousness. So the state has to change, as we have already covered in the fundamentals of breathing in Chapter Eight. Here I want to introduce you to a technique that, if learnt, will not only deal with any first tee issues but could have a profound impact on your life in general.

Pick a focus word that has significant meaning for you, such as 'calm', 'free', 'flow' etc.

Sit in a comfortable position with a relaxed posture and close your eyes.

Allow muscles to start relaxing.

Breathe smoothly and naturally, repeating the focus word selected in step 1 with each exhalation.

Be passive. If other thoughts come along, just observe them and return to the focus word for 10 to 20 minutes.

Effective practice

The second area that I want to focus on is effective practice, which includes pre-tournament preparation, practice rounds and the event itself.

Golf is almost unique in its ability to compromise the belief that hard work and effort will produce results. In my experience numerous golfers have put a tremendous amount into becoming a great player, but very often with little to show but lots of frustration and fatigue. I am not for one moment saying that you don't have to work hard to become as good as you can be, but I'm convinced that the way most people go about improving their game actually keeps them stuck at a poor level of development. Again, another unique aspect to golf is that we spend most of our practice time in an environment (the range), which has as much similarity to the golf course as a squash court has to a tennis court.

Effective practice should really only fall into one of two categories: improving mechanics, or simulating 'game' conditions. It's very important to understand that we will always have to keep working on our mechanics to some degree. The idea of 'train it and trust it' is an appealing one, but unfortunately recent scientific research on how our brain stores our swing suggests that we will never totally train our swing precisely into our neural networks.

Because of the design of the golfer, golf is a game of misses, as we have seen, and the player with the best misses wins. This information absolutely confirms two issues: we will always need the assistance of a trusted coach or the use of video to check our swing, and we will also need to develop the mental toughness to deal with a swing that to some degree or other will always let us down.

The key factor, so often missing in most players, is to know very clearly which kind of practice you are undertaking at any given time, and to have an equal balance between the two kinds. For most golfers, the practice that they do is an ill-defined, random mixture of both, leading to an ill-defined, random mixture of results. It is also true to say that we can only improve and move forward when we actually know where we are now. It is absolutely essential that the player has at his disposal a way of evaluating all aspects of his current game.

Other research suggests that overconfidence is also very prevalent where people can often dramatically overestimate their true capabilities. We have already discussed the need to build up a person's self-image, but this building of confidence must never be confused with establishing competence.

Make sure that you have at your disposal information on your game, the fairways you hit, the greens in regulation, putts, up and downs, sand saves. This is no different from monitoring a business profit and loss – you wouldn't want to just guess where your time and money was being spent!

To simulate game conditions, we have to put in the component parts that will be present when we actually play the game, namely: target, shot routine, variation and, most importantly, an element of concentration.

Concentration

Darren: It's interesting to see how people view concentration. Most will say they need it for golf, but if you ask them what concentration actually is, or how you achieve it, they have little or no idea of how to go about it. A lot of golfers seem to think that having a scowl on their faces and looking extremely serious is what concentration is about. They couldn't be further from the truth, as I have come to understand – concentration and having fun go hand in hand. They are a joint package.

When you're enjoying yourself you are generally concentrating, whether you're watching a film, or enjoying a great meal, or having a good conversation. As a contrast, think of the times in school when you were ordered to concentrate during a lesson so boring it made you feel you were beginning to lose the will to live! I also have a clearer idea now that concentration is not just about switching on – it's perhaps even more of a skill to switch it off.

Karl: Many players I work with complain at the beginning that they lack focus and ability to concentrate over the period of a round of golf. They look back on many rounds where they have simply thrown shots away, hit the ball almost without thinking, and let yet another game slip away into oblivion. Many times they walk off the course saying they are 'absolutely drained'. But are they physically or mentally tired?

One of the critical errors most golfers make is holding on to the mistaken belief that golf demands serious concentration for the entire round they play. This is a big mental error. Our ability to focus on our shots depends on being able to enter or leave an intense state of concentration.

The egg-timer of concentration

Now imagine that you go out on to the golf course with an egg-timer full of focused concentration, but that egg-timer can only contain about 90 minutes' worth of concentration.

Your future progress at golf will to a large extent depend on your ability to develop the skill of using the egg-timer at the appropriate time, and then being able to give yourself a mental break during the other periods of play rather than burning up your mental energy at the wrong time.

Each shot in golf requires approximately 40 seconds to plan and execute. Some recovery shots take longer, while some routine shots like tap-ins take significantly less, but the average comes to about 40 seconds. If you shoot par (70), that equates to 2,800 seconds of planning and executing (40 seconds $\times$ 70 strokes). This works out at about 45 minutes, which means that a round of golf requires significantly less than one hour of intense concentration.

We would have absolutely no problem in keeping our attention fixed for 45 minutes of a riveting conversation or a really good book, so why is it that we are so desperately poor with our concentration levels at golf?

I am pretty sure we can find some answers if we look to other sports. Consider football, for instance. What happens when two teams run out on to the pitch? They loosen up and get ready, but they don't start the game until they hear a certain signal – the referee's whistle. When it blows, letting them know it's time to play football, they play for 45 minutes (give or take a couple of minutes), and keep on playing until they hear the signal to stop (referee's whistle). It's half-time, they go in and have a break, listen to the manager, and then come out on to the pitch again.

Maintain your egg-timer of concentration. Learn how to switch on and off.

They don't start to play football again until they hear another signal, yes, the referee's whistle. You get the idea now - another 45 minutes and then again the referee sounds the final whistle.

Pretty much the same kind of thing occurs when playing tennis. After you have played two games you sit down, have a break, and then after a set period the umpire calls 'time'. It is significantly easier for both the footballer and the tennis player to focus their attention than it is for a golfer, because their attention span and concentration periods are dictated by referees, umpires and whistles, whereas in golf we don't have any real 'signals' to our brain that tell us when it's time to play golf and, more importantly, when that particular job (the shot) is now over.

Is it any wonder that golfers burn vital mental energy at the wrong time (in between shots) when they really need a mechanism to switch on and off their concentration?

The really good news is that the mind can be conditioned beautifully to react to certain specific signals if it's trained to do so. A red traffic light would mean absolutely nothing to someone who had lived his life in the Masai Mara game reserve. But when we see a red light we don't consciously slam on the brakes. Our foot just goes out to the pedal because we have conditioned ourselves to respond to that particular stimulus.

In golf we must create specific signals or anchors that tell our brain, 'Now I am playing golf', and when the shot is done, 'That's gone, over, finished.' This will become effective and automatic, especially if we link it to multi senses.

You will develop certain aspects that are personal to you within your routine, but I am convinced that you must create start signals and end signals at either end of the routine. Many times in sports psychology we hear the cliché 'to stay in the present moment'. That's all well and good, but you need a system to do that.

The start and end signals have the effect of focusing the mind in the present moment, and letting go after each and every shot.

Pressing your own buttons

What signals could you use to start your routine and get your mind to trigger a state of focused concentration? Perhaps it could be the sound of the Velcro on your glove, or a conscious deep breath, or a rattle of the clubs. Verbal start cues could be 'Ready', 'Focus', or 'Let's go'.

Now imagine that you have picked a start signal and a verbal cue to begin your routine. Close your eyes and imagine yourself on the golf course. You are walking down the fairway and you get to your ball. You fire off your start signal and cue word, and you notice that you go into a relaxed state of focus, absolutely ready to play the shot at hand. You know now that each time you fire off your signal to start, your mind will go into just that right state. That is the way that our brains work. Once we link or associate one stimulus with another, the brain will then keep going in that direction. This is exactly what Pavlov hit upon the best part of a century ago with his dogs and bells.

You need to follow exactly the same process to set up your end signal. That lets your brain know you have finished that particular task, and that your intensity of focus can shift to a more outward, relaxed mode. End signals could be something like the feel of the club going back into the bag, or taking your glove off, or a conscious deep breath. End verbal cues could be 'That's done', 'Finished', or 'Completed'.

It's vital that this aspect should be ingrained into your new mental approach. At first it will seem somewhat forced, but once ingrained it will be of huge benefit and, more importantly, will become permanent. But having created a beginning and end stimulus response, you will need to cater for your individuality within the routine. One system definitely does not work for all, so explore and find out what start and end signals work best for you personally.

Great decisions:
The fast track to lower scoring

Darren: When I think of all the different winners I see each year out on tour, all with different golf swings and methods of playing the game, it's hard to come up with a technical formula for success. But I do know that to be successful at any level at this game you have to make good decisions which match up to your ability level. Time after time I have seen amateur golfers attempt ridiculously difficult shots which even a top player would shy away from. If the average club golfer had one of the best tour caddies to make his decisions, I truly feel that he would instantly shave a couple of strokes off his handicap. I now understand that it's not just playing badly that can cause poor decision-making; when we are playing well there's a temptation to think we're invincible and to take on shots that are just not feasible. On tour we have the advantage of quality caddies who, if they are strong enough, will forcibly insist on the correct shot selection.

For your own game's sake, make a conscious commitment to better decision-making. This doesn't mean that you should play safe all the time, far from it, but what you can do is base your decisions on quality rational thinking. One thing I can guarantee is that good decisions do equal good scores.

Poor swings or poor decisions?

Karl: Often when a golfer is recalling a round of golf which has cost him a tournament, cheque, or prize, and is describing the shots he has hit, I will ask him, 'How many really bad swings did you make out there?' He might answer, 'Six bad swings.' And then I will ask him, 'How many bad decisions did you make?'

Usually the answer to the second question is similar in numbers to the first. When I then ask, 'If your decision-making improved by 50 per cent, what effect would that have on your scores?' The count on that one is usually pretty high! So what would be easier, to try to improve your swing by 50 per cent, or your decision-making by 50 per cent?

This is not to say that good decisions will overcome bad swings. You can make a great decision, but if you put an awful swing on the ball you will still end up in the water. However, it's my experience that most golfers give little or no attention to the decision-making process. Often when they have a club in their hand, and set up to the ball, they may wonder why they feel so uncomfortable – yet they still hit the shot. That uncomfortable feeling is very often down to your conscious and unconscious mind being at odds with each other, because a part of you 'knows' that you are just playing the wrong shot for you and your level of ability.

The critical element to this is that many golfers with poor decision-making skills actually have the club in their hand before they have done any sort of planning for the shot. This can often be attributed to the amount of golf they play on their home course when they are developing their game.

If we play the same course all the time, we get so used to the kind of shots we play that there is next to no decision-making process. We see the shot, pull out the club, and hope for the best, because that's exactly what we have done over and over again. We may develop as golfers, playing increasingly different courses, but our decision strategies often stay rooted in those early developmental days.

As we have already discussed, our mind affects our body and our body affects our mind. If we had to describe what thinking was like without using words, we would probably conjure up an image of 'the Thinker', head turned to one side, right hand on the chin. Or if we think of Jack Nicklaus making a decision before selecting a club, we can vividly imagine Jack in a certain pose as he allows his logical faculty to decide what shot to play.

Getting somewhat technical about this, we could say that good logical decisions on the golf course are preferably made with the left side of the brain, the analytical side, while the actual execution of the shot requires deployment of the right, more creative, side of the brain. Many golfers get this formula the wrong way around. They make very irrational but possibly creative decisions about what shot to play, and then tie themselves in knots by becoming extremely technical and far too left-brained about how to actually perform the swing.

To get you into making good decisions, I want you to take up what we call the 'decision pose' with the bag at your side, but without taking out a club. As you take up your decision pose, let this thought run through your mind: 'What is the absolute best way to play this shot in these circumstances?'

As you stand in your decision pose, you will be engaging the logical and analytical part of your mind, the part you need for good rational decisions. When good decisions are made, you can set up over the ball and regularly experience what I call the 'go signal' – that wonderful feeling we have when we 'know' the shot is going to come off. The 'go signal' does not appear when we have made a poor decision.

It's so very important for you to recognise what game you are actually playing out on the golf course. Are you playing scoring golf, or are you playing exhibition golf? The only criterion for scoring golf is to shoot as low as possible, while the criterion for exhibition golf is to impress other people, so that you go for spectacular shots and are prepared to suffer the consequences.

As long as you know which game you are playing you can then plan accordingly.

Many players are actually playing exhibition golf when they think that they're playing scoring golf, because at the unconscious level it is exhibition golf that's driving the show. Like your swing concept, your golf game will only be as good as your concept of what a good golf game should be.

If your concept of the game is hitting pretty shots, impressing others, gaining respect, or hitting the ball further than the next person, then you'll focus all your energies towards that goal, and scoring will be an afterthought. This usually leads to some pretty awful planning, and some extremely poor outcomes.

Scorers prioritise for low scores, and use the swing as a vehicle to get there. By stating exactly what kind of golf you have committed to, you will on the day be able gain clarity of intent, which is very powerful. When you set your frame of mind for the day to playing scoring golf, then your decision-making and focus take on a different dimension.

As part of your planning, decide what score you need and what score you can't survive, determine where you have to position the ball to make the score that you need, and eliminate the area that produces big numbers.

An essential element of superior planning is to know how you rate in relation to the field you are playing against. For example, when the wind blows, a lot of players feel they are losing ground if they make a couple of bogeys. They start to press, and usually shoot themselves in the foot by trying to pull off the impossible in difficult conditions.

The player who can read the field knows that a strong wind will affect everybody, and will actually raise the effective par for the day. An expert at planning and managing the course will realise that par 72 becomes more like 76 when the wind is blowing strongly. This prevents him from making rash decisions in an attempt to stay even with par 72.

Sometimes when you play too safe with one shot, you set yourself up for an extremely difficult and dangerous next shot. For instance, if you hit a three iron off the tee, when in fact you should only have dropped down to the three wood, you will then be faced with a second shot possibly using a long iron when the green is designed to take a medium iron, even if you hit a great tee shot.

When you know that the shot facing you is 'in-between clubs', it is vital to build your shot plan around your natural swing tempo. A fast-swinging power hitter will be far more committed to the shot if he takes one club less and hits it harder, but a smooth swinger will generally improve his success rate if he takes one club more and swings easy.

It is absolutely amazing how many golfers make a mess of the 'in-between shots' because they don't match up their club selection to their swinging style. For a fast swinger to be easing off a shot is usually a recipe for disaster.

Play to your strengths: a checklist

If possible, go with the shape of shot that you trust.

Attack and defend relative to your play on the day. Many golfers attack when playing poorly – a major mental error.

Never attempt a shot on the course that you haven't practised and hit well on the driving range.

Keep focused on any lay up shot. Give it your full intention and attention, as with any other shot.

Never make the mistake of having to play two recovery shots in a row. Get the thing out of trouble. Safe means safe.

Avoid lay ups to an uneven lie. As a rule it's better to hit a five iron from an even lie than a seven iron when the ball is below your feet.

Never lay up to an 'in-between' distance. Even great players have difficulty when faced with a distance that is neither one club nor the other.

Always pick a target, and let that be the most important part of your plan. The fairway or green is not specific enough. Your target must be clear, distinct and as specific as you can make it: for example, the left centre of the fairway in line with the lower branches of the tree in the distance.

Never make a swing unless you are mentally engaged and physically relaxed.

Arousal level: Setting the correct temperature

Darren: We hear a lot in sport these days about 'being up for it', or 'fired up', when athletes describe how they feel prior to playing in a big tournament or match. But I have come to understand that being up for it can be both good and bad, because there's a fine line between being ready to play and just running around like a headless chicken.

It's a little bit like the temperature on your car, which needs to hover inside a certain range, neither too hot nor too cold, to operate efficiently. In the past, especially at majors, my own temperature gauge has tended to run a little too hot; I end up trying to do too much and in effect become over-prepared.

This is an area that mostly comes down to knowing yourself and the type of person that you are. Do you need to fire yourself up? Or is it a case of playing things down and seeing it as just another tournament? Take some time to think about what is your best level of arousal. Think in terms of a gauge where the figure 1 is so laid back that you are almost horizontal, while 10 is so fired up that your eyes are beginning to bulge. Go back over some of your previous tournaments and get a sense of where you were on that scale prior to playing.

Getting it just right

In golf, arousal and stress levels usually need to be reduced rather than increased, unlike what may have to be done in coaching rugby players or boxers. For peak performance, golfers need to be mentally engaged and physically relaxed. The ability of our muscles to respond to the commands from the brain regarding the motor programme called 'golf swing' largely depends on the absence of tension and the presence of relaxation. Also, the ability to produce vivid mental images of intended outcomes will be drastically affected by our stress levels.

The stress response, the mechanism diametrically opposed to the relaxation response, is a centuries old, hard-wired internal response that tells our body to fight or to run away. It's a wonderful survival mechanism for fleeing from tigers, but useless if we want to shoot low scores.

Often a player will feel really tense as he sets up and grips the club, but to try to reduce tension at this point is far too late. We need to actually install the relaxation response much earlier in the routine. As you are going through your shot routine, take a deliberate deep diaphragmatic breath (We have already discussed the effect of deep breathing on state control) as you take the club out of the bag and before any practice swing; and use a cue word like 'Calm' or 'Relaxed'.

If this is done systematically, it will trigger the relaxation response and will provide a mechanism to help those of you with high anxiety levels. Another problem with over-arousal is the inability to produce good images of your target or ball flight. In general, being more relaxed will help you form clear images of what you want the ball to do.

The power of images

Images cue your muscles, and are powerful tools used by champions in all fields of sporting endeavour. Through imagery the past can be brought to life, the present enhanced, and the future created. The ability to produce multi-sensory images before each golf shot is a key to golf excellence.

Though imagery is a natural function of our brain, most golfers don't utilise this wonderful power source to good effect. Their images are either weak and dull, with limited effectiveness, or else they are strong, compelling images of failure.

NUGGET

A generation of American golfers grew up trying to copy Jack Nicklaus's upright swing, but how many really took to heart one of Nicklaus's most revealing insights published in *Golf my Way* in 1974.

'Setting up is 90 per cent of good shot making, I think it is the single ,most important manoeuvre in golf. Precise shot making is 50 per cent mental picture, 40 per cent set up and 10 per cent swing.

'I never hit a shot, even in practice, without having a very sharp, in-focus picture of it in my head. It's like a colour movie. First I "see" the ball where I want it to finish, nice and white and sitting up high on the bright green grass. Then the scene quickly changes and I "see" the ball going there: the path, trajectory and shape, even its behaviour on landing. Then there's a sort of fade-out, and the next scene shows me making the kind of swing that will turn the previous images into reality. Only at the end of this short, private, Hollywood spectacular do I select a club and step up to the ball.'

So it's extremely important for you to develop the skill of imagery as part of the shot routine. It is absolutely amazing that up to the present day this skill has not been taught in any sort of systematic way. The golfer is often told to 'visualise the shot' and then just left to it. The physical equivalent of this piece of advice would be to tell him to just 'swing the club on plane' and then leave him to it without any further instruction.

Imaging techniques need to be learnt, and the earlier the better. The power of the image will to a large degree be dependent on whether it is an associated or a dissociated image. If we see the action on our mental screen as though we were watching a movie of ourselves, then this would be a dissociated image, but if we encounter the action as if looking through our own eyes actually 'in' the image, then this would be an associated image.

A dissociated image is better than no image at all, but acquiring the skill of associated imaging will have much more impact on performance. If you could imagine seeing a video of yourself on a rollercoaster you might get a few butterflies in your tummy. But if you went right back to a time when you were actually there, and could feel yourself gripping the safety rail tightly, your heart pounding in your chest, and people screaming around you as you looked over the edge of the big drop ... You get the idea!

The absolute ideal in golf is to have a multi-sensory associated image of the shot we intend.

Not everyone we work with will be primarily visual in the way that they produce images. Some players will be more attuned to sound images, while others will work more from feel. But it has been my experience that if you develop one aspect of the senses with imagery, the others will follow.

For instance, some players we worked with could see no pictures whatsoever when they tried to imagine the ball in flight, yet when we had them describe the shot they wanted verbally inside, the images started to appear. The key aspect to all of this is to recognise that you are unique, and need to work with the components of imagery to find out what works best for you.

Practice swings and setting up

Almost all players go through the ritual of practice swing motion in some form, yet extremely few actually utilise the practice swing to produce any benefit whatsoever to their game. What is the purpose of the practice swing, and what are we looking to achieve? If we look at another discipline, acting in the theatre, we will be able to come up with some answers.

When a bunch of actors are given their parts in a play, they first of all read through the script on their own. Then they get together with players who will be involved in the same scenes, and read from their scripts in their normal everyday clothes. On the day before the actual performance they have the dress rehearsal, performing the play in costume, with the intention of coming as close to the real thing as possible. The dress rehearsal is a simulation of the real thing. The function of this is to train their acting brain for exactly what they wish to produce on the opening night. It gives their brain precise instructions as to what to produce.

What has this got to do with golf? Many players we see taking their practice swings are standing there, stopping and holding, checking positions halfway back, looking at the club. But this only confuses the brain because it doesn't quite know whether we are still on the practice range focusing on swing mechanics, or on the course and wanting to send a ball to a target.

Stopping and checking, and holding positions, is fine on the range when the focus of our intention is to create mechanical changes; but out on the course this is useless. The brain is a very literal instrument, and as such needs precise instructions for whatever you wish it to carry out.

A practice swing should be like the actor's dress rehearsal. It should get as close as possible to the actual action that you wish to perform. If I see someone from 200 yards away performing their dress rehearsal practice swing in real earnest, then I should be fooled into thinking that a ball could be on its way.

A really good dress rehearsal swing gives the brain extremely precise instructions, and it is also the opportunity to 'programme in' any mechanical swing thoughts that you may be working with, and which you really don't want cluttering up your mind when you are performing the shot.

Another reason why practice swings are so ineffective is that the player leaves both the ball and the target out of their rehearsal. Instead of a meaningless swing that bears no relation to the target or ball, try to create a perfect replica of the swing you intend, complete with all the elements and sensations that are part of your real swing, including imaging ball contact and flight. This full-blown dress rehearsal provides a powerful neurological route map which cues your muscles to perform the action you require.

Obviously, taking correct alignment is something that is taught essentially in the basics of learning to play good golf, but there are a couple of issues worth mentioning in terms of integrating this vital aspect of the game into your shot routine.

Whatever else golf may be, it certainly is a game of physics and geometry – with swing planes, lines and arcs that relate to you and your swing. The big problem is that the majority of golfers misalign to the right. Misaiming occurs when you approach the ball from the side. Because we have two eyes in the front of our head as opposed to the side, trying to sight the target from this oblique angle distorts your vision and your ability to aim relative to the target. The only way that you have a real chance of lining up correctly is to approach the ball from directly behind the target.

For correct alignment always approach the ball from behind.

Placing the bag

A key factor in this is where to position your bag when you come to play the shot. The number of golfers who place their bags level and to the right side of the ball is amazing. Make sure you have placed the bag behind the ball so that you will have the opportunity to approach the shot during the alignment process from directly behind the ball.

Another element that leads to misalignment is the result of practice habits. While on the range, you will see most players hit a shot, scrape another ball, hit a shot, scrape another ball, and so on, without ever checking their alignment. This is a recipe for misalignment once out on the course. Part of the function of practice should be a simulation of game conditions, and part of game conditions is the ability to line up correctly.

During your practice it's absolutely vital that part of your time is spent going through your actual on-course routine, and developing the habit of approaching the ball from behind.

When you have misaimed, the only way to hit a good shot is to make a bad swing by introducing compensations into your swing to cover the alignment error. If you make a good swing with bad alignment, your ball will miss the target. This is what is known as a distorted feedback mechanism where good swing equals bad shot, and bad swing (compensation) equals good shot. This is a nonsensical system, because how can we develop as players technically and mentally if this is going on? To avoid this crazy loop, keep having your alignment checked by your caddie or your friends, laying clubs on the ground or whatever you need to do to keep on top of this vital component of the game.

The time in between

Darren: One of the many roles that a truly great caddie takes on during a round of tournament golf is to act as friend and counsellor during the massive amount of time not spent in playing the game itself. It is this 'in-between' time that makes golf such a mental game. It is so easy to go inside your own shell and begin to dwell on mistakes, bad swings, bad luck, or whatever else your mind chooses to focus on. I think that in the future much more time will be devoted to developing the necessary mental skills in this huge part of the game.

Karl: Most, if not all, golf instruction concerns itself with the actual time you are playing golf, the shot routine part. If an average round of golf takes four hours, which is 240 minutes, and each shot takes about 40 seconds to play, as we have already worked out (see p.97), this means a round of 72 would come to 72 × 40 seconds, or about 48 minutes of play. That leaves 192 minutes on the course, more than three hours, when you are doing something other than playing golf.

It would seem almost insane to assume that, in an activity going on for 240 minutes, 192 minutes of that activity will have no affect on the remaining 48 minutes. Yet that is the way that golf is coached. How many of you have ever had a lesson on the in-between – the 192 minutes when you are not playing?

Working on what you do with yourself and your mind during this 'in-between time' will radically alter your golfing experience, and just might impact on your score. If you are like most of my clients, you probably take the opportunity to use that time to beat yourself up and drain off valuable mental energy from your egg-timer.

When I film clients in between shots, they are often absolutely amazed at what they see. Is this miserable, grumbling, slouched figure someone who is supposed to be enjoying himself and attempting to play golf to the best of his ability? And what they see after they have hit a bad shot often appals them.

Important conversations

We all talk to ourselves all day long, each and every day. Many of these conversations in our heads go unnoticed, but be sure that they have an effect. They affect the way we feel, the way we move, and the way we perform. Our self-talk may be in spoken words or unspoken thoughts. It can take the form of feelings, impressions, or even wordless physical responses – the knot in the stomach that comes when we are surprised or afraid, or the rush that comes with excitement or joy. We are thinking machines that never shut down.

Having control over our self-talk can be the difference between one bad shot leading to an absolute catalogue of disasters, or the ability to stabilise a round in the face of the inevitable errant shots. It can be the difference between starting the round steadily or being a complete mess on the first tee. It can be the fine line between closing out a tight match on the 18th and collapsing completely when the chance of victory is presented.

Much of our understanding of the importance of self-talk is based on the work of Dr Martin Seligman, one of the world's leading psychologists, who proved through scientific testing that the way people explain to themselves the good and bad events in their lives has a profound impact on their effectiveness in the world.

In his studies, Dr Seligman could go so far as to predict performance statistics with teams in baseball and basketball, based on their explanatory styles. My own experience is that most golfers have dreadful self-talk, and are always one shot away from beating themselves up mentally. The way that they relate to themselves during the round is often extremely counterproductive. Now, the way that you think is habitual, no different from habitually lining up badly. The good news is that both the ability to line up correctly and the way we habitually think can be changed for the better.

How do you think about the causes of the misfortunes, small and large, that befall you? Some people, the ones who give up easily, habitually say of their misfortunes, 'It's me, it's going to last forever, it's going to undermine everything I do.' Others, those who resist giving in to misfortune, say, 'It was just circumstances, it's going away quickly anyway, and, besides, there's much more to life.' Your habitual way of explaining bad events, your explanatory style, is more than just words you mouth when you fail, it is a habit of thought. These thoughts, these cognitions, determine whether our tendency is one of pessimism or optimism.

The power of memories

Karl: Just take a moment now to recall what you were doing on 9 April 2001. Unless that date has some specific association for you, like a birthday or an anniversary, you will probably, like most people, struggle to remember what happened that day. If you took out your diary and reviewed your appointments for that day, something might start to come back to you, but in the main it would be quite an effort.

Now recall what you were doing on 11 September 2001. You will find that not only can you remember the terrible events of that day, but also exactly where you were and who you were with. The memory will be vivid and precise, for many of us too vivid and too precise.

But why is that? Two dates in our own personal history, one completely vivid and easy to recall, the other a distant fading memory. This is a graphic example of our two forms of memory. One of them is charged with an emotion, and this memory is instantly recalled and extremely powerful. As the memory is recalled, we instantly have a physical reaction to it.

What has this got to do with your golf? Well, maybe everything. If the above example tells us that we have a dual coding system of events, and that events associated with strong emotions will be instantly recalled, then we need to be extremely careful about how we use our emotions on the course, and how we process that experience afterwards. Think what golfers generally do after they have completed a round. They invest their emotions heavily in the negative events that have occurred, and only pay lip service to the good events.

We so often see players 'blowing up' after a bad shot, getting really annoyed with themselves, the course, the caddie and anything else that comes on the radar of their attention. What they do not realise is that they are inadvertently laying down tracks of failure for the future as the brain instantly recalls the negative emotions that will influence later play.

We don't have to blow up externally either. Many players internally attach huge emotion to bad shots, beating themselves up, and moaning and whining at their own perceived lack of talent. This is a more sinister and covert method of destroying our ability. And it is a way of laying down neural connections in our brain that will keep us repeating the same errors over and over again.

In simple terms, if we start to attach more emotion to our successful outcomes, and reduce the emotional charge on less than desirable shots, then we will literally start to re-wire the circuitry in our brain, and start to change our own beliefs about our golfing capability.

This information explains so many of the seemingly illogical occurrences we encounter at golf. Why is it that we get on to a certain hole and always play it well, yet on another hole we make a consistent hash of it? On certain courses we only need to turn into the driveway and we know that we're going to have a good day, but when we come face to face with a particular opponent we know that we are going to get beaten.

All these examples are evidence of the way our memory storage for past events has a huge influence on our performance. These emotionally charged memory traces will overcome any 'good form' we take into a given day, and will continue to wreak their own brand of unwanted havoc. In many ways we are conditioned to do this from a very early age because, as we have seen, in school it is primarily our mistakes that are highlighted. Through our entire lives we are exposed to society's habitual need to focus on what is missing or what is at fault rather than what we get right. Newspapers and magazines sell many of their editions by pointing out what's wrong with the world.

In golf it's so easy to really focus on what we have done wrong and give little or no attention to the things that we do well. The normal coaching approach tends to focus on our faults. But this is not true of the great players, for they have the ability to develop what I call 'selective amnesia'. They find a way of reducing the emotional charge attached to a bad event, and increasing the emotional reaction to good events, as we saw earlier when we referred to Jack Nicklaus's amnesia concerning short putts.

NUGGET

What I want you to do is to get really high inside when you hit a good shot, maybe make a specific gesture to yourself when you hit the ball exactly as you planned, something simple like clenching your fist or sqeezing the grip on the club.

What you will be doing here is actually creating a positive association in your brain to the good shots. You will be increasing your mental library of positive experience but linking it neurologically with a specific motion and a high dose of emotion. You will literally be creating in your brain neural pathways or tracks of your own excellence. These tracks will then hugely influence your future performance.

Have you ever noticed that when Tiger hits a good shot he gives the club a little twirl after the ball has gone? Well, he is anchoring that good shot to that gesture, linking that good shot in his brain. He doesn't twirl the club if the shot is not what he requires, he just lets that go.

What we have here is an opportunity for you to implement a very specific, highly advanced, way of running your golfing brain. As you continue to process your outcomes this way you will find that your game can and will evolve to a new level. You may also be pleasantly surprised at the fact that you seem to be enjoying your time out on the course significantly more than you have done for a long, long time.

These techniques are not instant cures or quick tips, but life skills that take a period of time to implement and then to bear fruit. But the investment of your time and commitment will be rewarded very handsomely. The first time you do this there will be no effect whatsoever, nor will there be with the second or third. But after a couple of hundred times you will be a different person on the golf course, your brain will have literally changed the way that it 'codes' the activity known as golf. This is the challenge to you. Rise to the challenge, because this stuff works.

Above This is what you hit all the balls in practice for. Winning the Ryder Cup is an indescribable feeling.

Right No time to be thinking about your technique. Paul McGinley focused on the process not the outcome to hole the winning putt in the Ryder Cup.

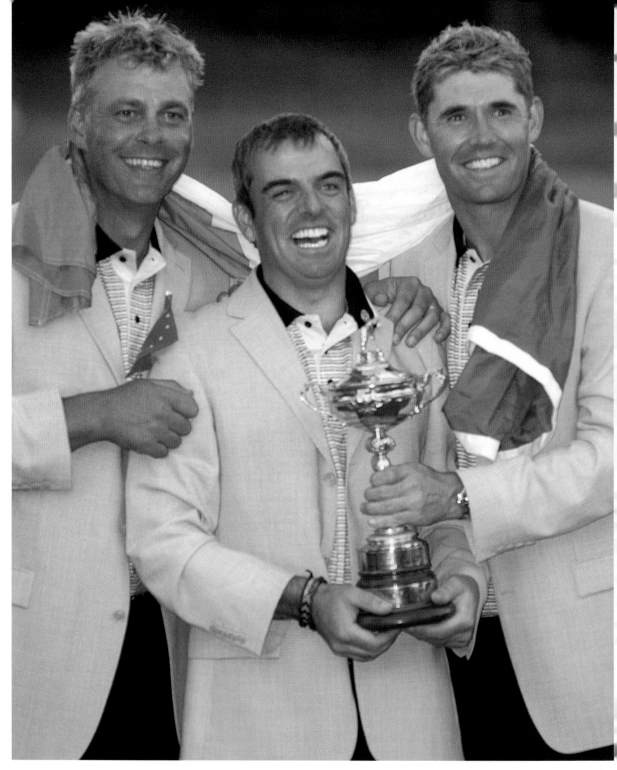

The victory can be short-lived, so savour the moment. Padraig Harrington and I on either side of Paul McGinley after the Ryder Cup Victory at Oakland Hills, 2004.

Nick Faldo worked with a sports psychologist in the early eighties, back when nobody talked about the mental game.

Right Seve Ballesteros was a genius for creating incredible recovery shots with the power of imagination.

Left Jack Nicklaus – still focused on the target well into his sixties.

Below 'Sensing victory'. Looking forward to 'that feeling' on the back nine on the Sunday of a Major – Jack Nicklaus in his prime.

Left Getting hot with the putter – the 'other' game that is almost all mental once you have a workable technique.

Right Retief Goosen has a great temperament for the game. A calm, neutral mind is hard to beat.

Below Paul Casey had a difficult relationship with the Americans. It's a tough game anyway but almost impossible when you are distracted by other issues.

Graeme McDowell has worked very hard with Karl, rising from ninety-sixth to sixth in the 2004 European Order of Merit.

Store the good shots in your memory bank. Relive your success vividly.

Getting beliefs to work for you

Darren: I have been fortunate to play with or meet some of the greatest golfers to have ever played the game, and one thing they all seem to have in common is belief, total and utter belief in themselves and their ability, even when their game has been less than 100 per cent. It doesn't matter whether it's a swing change, a fitness programme or a new putter, having belief and faith is absolutely critical. Perhaps the greatest example of belief is Gary Player, whom I have spent some time with. This is a man who has achieved incredible feats in the game as a result of total conviction that what he was doing was going to make him into a great player.

Karl: Is there any discipline in the world of sport that is so dominated and affected by one's beliefs as the game of golf? If we consider the nature of the game and the way our mind plays such a vital role in how we perform in tournaments, it becomes painfully clear that the beliefs that we carry around the course with us will to a large extent determine our golfing destiny.

Thinking about the greats of the game, such as Tiger Woods, Annika Sorenstam, Karrie Webb and Ernie Els, do they not represent the very embodiment of belief in themselves? How many times have we heard people say, 'She would go a long way if only she would believe in herself,' or, 'He just doesn't seem to believe in himself'? We see in such people all the necessary attributes for becoming a fine player, yet something just seems to be missing, that intangible final ingredient that provides the difference between success and just potential.

I often ask players what they are bringing with them to the first tee. If you press the question a bit, after the initial quizzical look and the obvious answers like 'golf clubs', 'balls', 'umbrella' etc, a picture starts to emerge of all the things they bring that are internal to them but will show up in the external world.

The beliefs, hopes and expectations for the day ahead will be among the many things that they bring with them. If a person brings to the tee a deeply held belief that he is inadequate against better players, then that belief will drive his behaviour at an unconscious but pervasive level. Even though his play is good enough to win, and opportunities to win come up during the game, the negative belief will at some point sabotage the effort and he will find a way to lose.

Believe in yourself

Tiger Woods' experience in his US Amateur days, when he captured the title three times, graphically illustrates this. Woods believed he could win, and although he definitely shouldn't have won some of the matches he played in the finals, his beliefs drove his behaviour. His opponents, on the other hand, probably didn't believe they could win, so the belief dominated their behaviour and they found ways of losing even when they really should have closed out the game.

The amazing thing about beliefs is that the mind will constantly seek to keep confirming the beliefs we hold. If I believe I'm a useless putter, at a deep level of consciousness my mind will keep creating behaviour to validate that belief. If I perform contrary to that belief, i.e. I hole some putts, the belief will act upon me by actually screening out those holed putts from my attention. It is almost as though the belief actually distorts my perceptions.

So even though I hole the putts, I don't really notice them. My mind is far more interested in waiting until there is more behaviour to confirm the original belief, saying, 'I holed a couple early on, but missed so many on the back nine.' My whole game will revolve around a series of beliefs, and while many of these will be supportive and assist me in playing to my potential, it is more than likely that certain beliefs will be getting in my way and limiting my development as player.

Instructors often give the player the advice to 'believe in your swing, just trust it'. But until we know more about the structure of our beliefs, how they operate and how we can adjust them to achieve our goals, then the advice to believe in something will remain just that, a piece of advice.

Beliefs send commands to our nervous system, so we need to be able to detect, adjust and install powerful supporting beliefs. The first step in understanding beliefs is to know the difference between a thought and a belief. I can certainly think a thought, we have thousands every day, and it will have little or no effect on me. It is just part of a stream of consciousness – 'This putter feels nice' – as opposed to a rock solid belief such as 'I am a great putter'.

What turns a thought into a belief? A thought becomes a belief when you confirm it, validate it, repeat it, confirm it, validate it, repeat it; and as you repeat this cycle over and over, the thought becomes solidified into a belief. Such is the power of this that we can see in the world today the good and bad that can be created if someone is conditioned to repeat an idea over and over until it becomes a solidly entrenched belief.

So for you and your game it is vital to recognise what you keep saying to yourself and confirming over and over again. Keep telling everyone that you're a useless bunker player and you will turn a perfectly harmless thought into a strong belief. By contrast, if you keep telling yourself that you're improving, if you keep writing down how you have improved, and imagining that you are improving even more, you may well find a new set of beliefs emerging, and a new level of confidence.

Be careful what you keep repeating ... You have been warned!

CHAPTER 26

The long ball:
Mind and body for
distance

Is there anything in the game of golf that gets us so fired up as the thought of ripping a drive miles down the middle of the fairway? Is there not a huge industry dedicated primarily to the quest for greater distance with clubs and balls? And what is the one club that most people want to use on the driving range? The driver, of course. There is something inherently pleasurable about seeing a golf ball climb and soar into the sky, and then seemingly carry on forever.

Yet in our quest for greater distance, what do we normally do? We may take some lessons, and the pro will talk about club head speed and winding the coil in the body, or we may buy a new driver, possibly even go down to the gym. One thing is for certain: we usually strain to hit it a bit further, our muscles tighten, and we force the swing, trying to use muscular strength to propel the ball greater distances.

We believe that all these standard approaches will generally end in frustration and failure. What the established approach usually creates is tension, which is an absolute killer to an effective golf swing. Tight muscles are actually very weak muscles.

Karl: In this context we can learn much from the eastern martial art disciplines, where so much attention is paid to creating relaxed, ready muscles set to perform efficient movement.

When we use the various muscle groups, they're powered electro-neurologically. The brain emits an electrical impulse that travels down the spinal column and shoots out to the muscles, activating the chemicals that cause the muscle to contract. If the muscles are not relaxed (oxygenated), or if they are in a state of tension (lack of oxygen), then the codes that you are putting into the brain will not have the opportunity to work effectively. Tension creates roadblocks to physical performance; relaxation enhances it.

Some of the techniques that we will discuss in this chapter may seem somewhat radical, and a break from what you are used to working on. All we ask is that you suspend your judgement until you have given them a try, and really enjoy the results you can achieve with their application.

From a very early age we are conditioned to believe that effort and power go together hand in hand. We see images from other sports of athletes straining and grunting their way through a movement, their faces contorted with strain and tension. Think of the language that we use: 'It took a superhuman effort.' 'Take the strain.' 'Try your hardest.'

All these phrases conjure up the idea that achieving a favourable outcome in sport involves great physical strain, and of course this tends to work its way into our golf. Yet how many of us have experienced that phenomenon of playing a shot with no effort in an attempt to lay up short of a green that we considered out of range, only to find the ball screaming off the clubface, and going miles further than we would ordinarily expect?

On these occasions were we tight and tense? Did we use much physical effort? The usual reaction is one of total surprise that the ball could have gone so far with such apparent ease. These experiences are a glimpse into the underlying principles of effortless power.

Effortless power

Darren: We all love to give the ball a whack and see it soar off into the distance. One of the strong points of my game is without doubt my driving. I have managed over the last few years to combine distance with accuracy by keeping my power under control. Make no mistake, though,

Tense muscles are weak muscles.

in the modern game power is an absolutely essential ingredient for success. Tiger, Ernie, Vijay, they all send the ball out there. Courses are getting longer and longer, and, without overstating the obvious, you are going to knock it much closer going in with your second shot wedge in hand than with a five iron.

Many amateur golfers I see and play with in pro-ams tend to go about hitting a long ball in totally the wrong way. But I think if you can grasp our concepts in this chapter you will find that your distance off the tee could be transformed without having to compromise on accuracy.

Karl: Effortless power at golf has three key components: relaxation, centring, and natural timing. If you took any one of these and worked with it, you would notice a difference in your distances. If you combined all three you would experience a phenomenal shift. All these principles have the added benefit of blending with the other points that we have made through this book; and you will also find that your added distance is in no way compromised by losing any accuracy. In fact we have found our results to be just the contrary: not only do the players we work with hit it further, they hit it straighter as well, not a bad combination.

Work with one principle at a time until it is integrated into your game. It shouldn't be at all long before you start to see noticeable changes and tangible results. You will probably notice these changes only on certain holes at first, but this will grow and grow as you gain faith in what you are experiencing.

If we had to choose one principle above all the others, almost a universal principle, it would be that of relaxation. When we talk of relaxation we mean total muscular relaxation, for we have a firm conviction that there is no place for tension in the pursuit of great golf.

Tension is like a shadow that constantly follows us around. We may have some sort of awareness of its presence, but we're not sure exactly where it is, and generally we have no idea how to get rid of it. Yet once we shine some light on the shadow through awareness and attention, it will then start to disappear.

Relaxation

Developing the skill of profound muscular relaxation is a lifelong pursuit, with rewards in every aspect of our life, not merely on the golf course. To relax, we must actually endeavour to make all our tissues completely supple, even limp. None of our joints should be locked. We must consciously direct this, and feel the body loosen and open. When we move, using relaxation as our principle, the movements that we make will seem unlike ordinary movement, the flow of your golf swing will take on a new dimension. One of the sources of power within a golf swing is to use the effects of gravity. The only way which you can use gravity to source your movement directly is to relax. You must relax into the earth, rather than resist it. No matter how relaxed you become, you can relax even more.

It has been demonstrated that deep muscular relaxation cannot co-exist with anxiety. Calm mind and calm body go hand in hand. Relaxation allows for greater speed, power, balance, and the opportunity of swinging the golf club in the most efficient manner possible.

Now take your normal golf stance and see if you can sense any tension in your body. Do an imaginary body scan, start at the top of your head and work your way own.

Notice if you have any tension in your face, arms, hands, grip, stomach, legs. Just allow your internal tension scanner to work its way all round your entire body. You may be quite surprised at what actually comes into your awareness. Do you detect certain areas of tension which had been hidden from you in the past?

As you notice the areas of tension, just allow yourself to tighten up these areas even more. Just increase the tension until you can feel those muscles really tight. Now, starting at the top of your body, just allow all of that tension to drain away. Imagine that the tension is a liquid, give it a colour, and imagine it's draining out of your body, flowing out of your legs, into the ground.

As it runs out you can detect a growing sense of calm flowing through your body from top to bottom. Get a feeling that even your joints are starting to relax and become supple. However relaxed you feel, relax even more, sense that you are almost sinking into the ground. Just let that tension completely drain away.

The next time you go to the range, allow yourself to go through the same process, and start by really noticing whatever tension is actually present. Increase it, increase it some more, and then just allow it to drain away, from the very top of your head, right out to the bottom of your feet. Let the tension flow into the ground. Now in this state make some swings. Notice how you feel. Let go of any judgements of what should and shouldn't be happening, just allow yourself to be. Notice how it feels to play golf in this state.

We know from scientific research that you cannot be anxious or fearful if you are in a state of deep relaxation; you need the physiology to support your anxiety. If you haven't got that physiology, your anxiety will collapse.

Centring

The second principle is that of centring. Have you ever noticed that great sports stars always seem to be in balance? No matter how frantic the play is, they always seem to have time to make the play. They seem to have a sense of what's happening even before the action actually occurs.

This balance is due to the concept of centre. All the great martial arts teachers place great importance on the ability to know and embrace your physical centre, which lies in a spot just below your navel. This is literally the centre of your body.

When we have our attention fixed on our centre, we can create an incredible balance and stability, providing the platform for great power and fluidity. Yet when we are playing golf, where do we tend to place our attention? Usually on the club, or on the extremities of our body, because so much of standard instructional focus is on the movements that are the farthest away from our bodies. But when we do this we immediately lose our sense of stability and balance.

A useful exercise is to place your conscious awareness upon your physical centre when you are on the practice tee after setting yourself up for your normal golf swing. Just allow your mind to rest in your centre. Take a practice swing, with your attention still focused on your centre. Notice your sense of balance as you make the movement. Become aware of the motion of your centre during your golf swing. Now hit some shots for real, and as you do this again keep your attention on your centre.

Is your movement any different from your practice swing? Is your sense of balance any different? What is the quality of your strike like with your attention on your centre? Now make a deliberately fast and aggressive swing. Notice how your sense of centre changes. This is a tremendously beneficial exercise, because by becoming aware of your centre you automatically become more balanced. By comparing your practice swing with your actual swing, and also with a swing that is too aggressive, you are really able to tune in to your body and listen to how it works at its most efficient.

Also, when you pay attention to your centre you are absolutely grounded in the present moment. The present moment is always the entry point to the zone.

The most amazing aspect of centring is its absolute simplicity. Over and over again I have seen astounding results with a person's golf swing when they let go of all their wasted muscular effort, place their attention on centre – and just discover.

Centring again asks you to suspend some of your logical judgements. It seems so natural to think that if we want to hit the ball a long way, we should be thinking of the club or our arms or legs, but as you suspend those judgements, let yourself just enjoy the experience. Let the results start to speak to you, not your previous beliefs and conditioning. I would almost go as far as to say that if a golfer did nothing other than learn the basic fundamentals, and then just consistently placed his attention and focus on his centre, he would become a very fine player.

Natural timing

We have noticed over the last few years that the final part of the power equation links the whole thing together, and that link is natural timing. This is something that you don't have to get, it's always there, and it's natural. We all have a sense of timing for just about everything we do: the way we walk, the way we talk, the way we dance, and the way we do sports.

The language people use to describe their best rounds of golf also gives us a good clue to the importance of natural timing: 'My swing just felt so easy today.' 'I was timing it sweet as a nut out there.' 'I found my timing on the back nine and, boy, did that thing go.'

The opposite is the case when we hear descriptions of a bad day at the golfing office: 'My timing just wasn't right today.' 'My back swing was way out of synch.' 'I felt some pressure and, boy, did that swing speed up.' The problem occurs, and in golf it is huge in the sense that with too much conscious processing, our natural timing gets knocked out.

Think now of the experience most golfers have when they take their first golf lesson: 'Get the grip right.' 'Make sure you're standing correctly.' 'Line up properly.' 'Now take the club back with a turn of your shoulders.' 'Do that really slowly.' 'All the way to the top.'

The conscious mind is absolutely overloading the body with do's and don'ts. Typically the swing is very forced and wooden on the back swing, then a wild slash at the ball on the downswing. The coach usually then says, 'You came out to in on that one. Get more on the inside next time.' More conscious overload. The real problem, though, is that this is the frame that is set for how you then play golf – always thinking and not enough doing.

Consider a similar situation: the person who stammers. Generally he is thinking about the words that he wants to say well before he says them. And guess what – his natural flow is interrupted. Something that is normally done without thought then becomes an ordeal.

Compare this with the way we can hold a piece of paper in our hands, screw it into a ball, look at a waste bin ten feet away, and then throw the paper so that it either goes in the bin or at least goes very close.

What we have just done there is actually pretty incredible! With one quick glance, the brain has computed how far away the bin is, how far we need to move our arm back, the speed of the back swing, and the precise speed of the release. How good would we be, though, if somebody tried to teach us those moves in the way that we're taught to play golf?

The overriding emphasis with conventional golf instruction is verbal input: Do this, don't do that. The problem is that the part of our brain that swings the golf club does not process verbal information, it responds to images and sensations. This is why children learn golf so wonderfully well; they just have a visual image generally, and they go out and copy that image. They don't have a constant stream of verbal commands being drilled at them before, during, and after the swing.

We feel that so many of the so-called errors in the golf swing are a direct result of natural timing being upset; but trying to fix the errors with more conscious thought about the error itself will only result in the error persisting. When you are able to rediscover your natural sense of timing, the so-called errors will disappear.

Again, the principles we are discussing here require you to suspend some of your entrenched beliefs on how golf should be taught. If you are happy with the results that conventional wisdom gives you, then fine. If not, you will be very pleasantly surprised.

How then do you rediscover your natural timing? The credit for this must go to a gentleman in southern California called Fred Shoemaker. Fred, who is an inner game coach, discovered the secret one day when he was waiting in between lessons on the coaching tee and just fooling around. He had an amazing insight, and as so often happens with these insights, it came to him when he was least expecting it.

Fred noticed that if he simply looked at a target in front of him with a golf club in his hands, and threw the club towards the target, he got a sense that the rhythm of each throw was exactly the same. With the curiosity of a true genius he then started to experiment with his pupils, asking each of them to simply throw some clubs at a target. He videoed each throw, and then with the frame timer on the camera started to calculate the speed of each person's throw or swing. The incredible thing was that the timing sequence for each part of each person's swing was exactly the same.

This compared interestingly with normal swings, where the timing was all over the place from swing to swing. Now what is the difference between the throw and a normal swing? The normal swing is full of conscious 'advice' and interference, while the throw just happens naturally.

The other interesting detail was that when most of the pupils' normal swings were timed, typically the back swing tended to be slow and forced, the start of the downswing really quick, and then the club stalling through impact ... sounds familiar? Yet the throw tended to be flowing on the backward movement, and then there was a gradual progressive acceleration into the point of release.

So could it possibly be that the body has an instinctive knowledge of how best to propel an object at maximum speed in the most efficient manner? Of course. When we connect with the part of us that actually knows how to do this thing called golf, then there is magic in the air.

We are confident of what we're saying here because, in spite of all the huge advances that there have been in golf, such as better equipment, better courses, video technology, more coaching, and so on, the average handicap in the United States has remained the same. Golfers are not getting better.

Many pros love to blame this on the fact that people don't practise, but it has been my experience over the years that many golfers are desperate to improve, taking many lessons, working hard on the practice tee, and yet getting absolutely nowhere.

The coaches, and the way golf is ordinarily taught, must shoulder some of the blame for this very sad statistic. Now, to get a sense of what we're talking about you need to get some old clubs and go to an open grass area where you won't be disturbed. Just pick a target a few feet in front of you and start to throw some clubs towards the target. While you do this, place your attention on the timing of the movement, allow yourself to step back into an observer position and just notice, free from any judgements of right or wrong, the speed of the movement. After you have done this, hit a few shots, and while you are still in the observer mode just notice if the timing of your swing is the same as the throw.

Do not repeat, do not try to copy the throw, because that would be going back to conventional coaching, and we know that doesn't work. Just stay in an awareness mode and see if you can detect any differences in the motion, and if so where they are.

As you begin to notice the differences, your brain will then reconnect with your natural sense of timing, something that you may have denied yourself from the very first time that you started to play golf. As your brain senses the differences, you will find that your normal golf swing will take on the qualities of the throwing swing.

For many of the people we have worked with, this is literally a life-changing experience in terms of their golf. After this experience they realise that there is no going back to the old model of coaching.

What is the point in continuing to put our faith in something that just does not produce the goods? Yet if we only know one way, then we will be trapped in the prison of familiarity and comfort even though, time and time again, it will have proved to be of little or no effective use.

The three principles that we have covered in this section, relaxation, centring, and natural timing, are simple yet profoundly effective. They can be used in so many different areas of our lives where performance issues are being raised. For many people it will be a challenge to let go of the need to try so hard to consciously control their golf swings, but again, as in so many other areas, don't we perform at our best when we just let go and trust?

It seems that we have been so conditioned by society constantly to question our own abilities through intellectual analysis. Intellect and analysis of course do have a valuable role to play in the world, but unfortunately if we bring too much of these qualities to bear upon our golf, the performance tends to suffer greatly.

The zone:
What is it and how do we
get there?

Roger Bannister on the first sub four-minute mile: 'I felt that the moment of a lifetime had come. There was no pain, only a great unity of movement and aim. The world seemed to stand still, or did not exist. The only reality was the next two hundred yards of track under my feet.'

John Brodie, former San Francisco 49er quarterback: 'A player's effectiveness is directly related to his ability to be right there, doing that thing, in the moment. All the preparation he may have put into the game - all the game plans, analysis of movies, etc. - is no good if he can't put it into action when game time comes. He can't be worrying about the past or future or the crowd or some other extraneous event. He must be able to respond in the here and now.'

Arnold Palmer describing his version of the zone: 'Tournament play involves a tautness of mind, but not a tension of the body. It has various manifestations. One is the concentration on the shot at hand. The other is the heightened sense of presence and renewal that endures through an entire round or an entire tournament. There is something spiritual, almost spectral about the latter experience. You're involved in the action and vaguely aware of it, but your focus is not on the commotion, but on the opportunity ahead. I'd liken it to a sense of reverie – not a dreamlike state but the somehow insulated state that a great musician achieves during a great performance. He is aware of where he is and what he is doing, but his mind is on the playing of the instrument with an internal sense of rightness – it is not merely mechanical, it is not only spiritual; it is something of both, on a different plane and a more remote one.'

How do we get there?

We hear so much these days about 'the zone', such as, 'I was playing in the zone.' Or, 'I just got lost in the zone.' So what is the zone, and how do we get there?

Descriptions of the zone we have heard over the years suggest that the experience is so inherently pleasurable, the actual feeling itself is so good, that many athletes seek to re-enter the zone for no other reason than to recapture those very special feelings, not necessarily to win a title or match. The winning seems to be a by-product of the experience itself. You hear statements like, 'Time just seemed to stand still.' 'I had so much time to make my swing.' 'I just knew that the shot was good before I even hit it.' These remarks seem to describe a very altered state of mind, and one that produces extraordinary results.

The strange thing about the zone is that you don't know you have been in it until you come out of it. You are so absorbed in the experience itself that you're not even aware that it's happening.

Complete absorption in any activity is what the mind truly seeks, almost as its natural state. If you think of activities like reading, watching sport, doing DIY, and so on, isn't it a feature of such hobbies that for a period of time we 'lose ourselves' in what we are doing? When the book is totally compelling, doesn't the plot seem so believable that for a period it becomes real for us? Again, we seem to have a distortion of time, which seems to fly past. But has time changed? Of course not, only our perception of the time.

Contrast this with the modern way of life. Isn't it the case that most of our normal states are the very opposite of a zone experience? Typically, we might be eating breakfast, listening to the news on TV, pretending to have a conversation with the person next to us, glancing

Put the ball in play! Focus like a tennis player on the second service, completely absorbed in the target area.

at the headlines in the paper, and at the same time previewing what an incredibly busy day lies ahead of us. But where is our mind? Literally all over the place.

We have been conditioned into a mindset which is the total opposite to that which we require for mastery, or even, at a more basic level, for the feelings of calmness and contentment that we all crave so much. Is it any wonder that the whole entertainment and leisure business is so huge? We're spending millions of dollars in the pursuit of brief periods of time when our mind is absorbed in something, to the exclusion of other distractions.

The monkey mind

In eastern meditation disciplines, the mind has been labelled the 'monkey mind' – a wonderful description of our busy western mind, flitting from one thought to the next like a monkey swinging from tree to tree, and chattering away endlessly. Many problems such as insomnia, aspects of depression, or inability to concentrate, can be explained by this 'monkey mind' concept, operating with such incredible busy-ness inside our heads, the thoughts constantly vying for space and attention.

Is it any wonder that when we get on to the golf course we find it difficult, if not impossible, to enter the zone? Yet might it be possible that golf itself could provide the environment where experiences profoundly affecting the rest of our lives could come to us? What if golf could be viewed as a 'medium' to develop aspects of concentration and a quietening of the mind? Golf does indeed provide many opportunities for us. It can be endlessly frustrating if the focus of our attention is distorted, or it can lead us to states of mind that give us such a sense of well-being and fulfilment, when the game becomes worth playing for its own sake, not just for the score on the bottom of the card at the end of the round.

No way are we saying that the score is irrelevant. But what we are constantly working on with our clients is how to go about achieving those results. For so many golfers the old ways of training, with lots of effort and trying so hard, are just not working. We are absolutely convinced that the first step in having experiences of the zone is an admission of its existence, and the possibility of having these experiences.

If you realise that there is a state to play golf in that is very different from our normal state, then you provide yourself with the opportunity of allowing that state to emerge. You cannot just switch on the zone like a light, but what you can do is set the scene for a zone experience to come out.

By following the suggestions and exercises outlined in this book you will provide yourself with the optimum in terms of the possibilities of zone experience.

Stop thinking –
and come to your senses!

Darren: When I first started to work with Karl I had never even considered the importance of what he calls the 'in-between' time, the period out on the course when you are not actually playing golf. As we have seen, 85–90 per cent of the game is 'in-between' time, yet all too often we focus almost completely on the technical aspect of the game. It is so obvious, I now understand, that what you do during the 'in-between' will have a massive impact on the actual time you are playing golf in terms of your ability to be focused and ready to play.

One thing is for certain: if you develop some of these skills that Karl is talking about, you will at the very least enjoy your golf and the experience of the game far more than you may ever have thought possible.

Pay attention

Karl: Next time you're in between shots on the golf course, notice how 'present' you are to your actual experience. Are you really seeing what's going on around you? Can you hear the sounds of the course? Are you aware of the feel of your feet as you walk along the fairway? Or are you in your head? Are you still playing the last shot on the last hole over and over? Or maybe you're thinking of the holes that you're about to play, or possibly what score you're about to shoot, good or bad.

All of this thinking takes us away from our direct experience; it takes us away from the very thing that we should be attending to and concentrating on. It takes us away from the present moment, the now.

When writers on sports psychology talk about being 'in the present moment', this is what they're alluding to. As one great teacher said, 'All the wisdom you will ever need you will find in the present moment.' But what the sports psychology writers very often do not do is tell you how to actually stay in the present.

Really focusing on your surroundings puts you back in touch with that present moment.

Golf is very different from many other sports in the fact that our attention should be on the playing of the shot for only a very small part of the time that we are out on the course. So many golfers mentally burn themselves out by trying to maintain an intense focus of attention for the whole four or five hours that they are out playing. This is just not possible.

An Olympic rifle shooter we were working with told us that in his opinion we probably only have about a couple of hours of intense focus within us in any given day. In his particular sport he had to be fully concentrated on the actual shot, and when he was in between shots he needed to mentally 'get outside of himself' so as not to drain too much out of his mental batteries.

Air traffic controllers are only allowed to work a couple of hours per day because of the levels of concentration required. In that job the consequences of losing your concentration are too terrible to contemplate. The point we are making here is that we only have the ability to focus intently for just so long.

Give your mind a break

With golf it's so important to get outside ourselves in between shots, to give ourselves a break ready for the next shot. How many times do we see players hit a really bad shot and then start to withdraw into themselves, their mood changing and their golf going to pieces? They are so much in their heads that when it's time to play the shot they have little or no mental reserves left. They have spent so much time thinking about golf when they are not playing that, when the time comes to hit the actual shot, their minds are still on the past bad hole or some perceived future scenario. So the quality of their attention in the present moment is extremely weak.

When Walter Hagen talked about 'taking time to smell the flowers' during a game of golf, he was making a profound statement, because when he did this he was literally practising being in the moment. Over the years his comment has been wrongly presented as just a devil-may-care attitude, but we believe that he knew, at a very instinctive level, that his mind needed that break in between shots, ready for the next challenge.

We have also been fed images of players like Ben Hogan seemingly locked in a world of total concentration. But we don't know how such players were really experiencing the world themselves, or what was really going on inside their heads.

Bjorn Borg, the Swedish tennis great, was always perceived as the 'Iceman', as though he had absolutely no emotion. But he later stated that this was his 'construction', his way of creating an outward persona to the world at large, which gave him the best chance of winning. Afterwards he let it be known just how great a time he was having out there. He just didn't show it outwardly.

On the golf course, what is absolutely certain is that you just cannot maintain laser focus continually for four or five hours, it's just not possible. Not only is it not possible, it's pretty boring too. There are a lot of wonderful times to be had in some wonderful locations, and not all of these revolve around actually hitting the ball, or the outcome of a particular shot.

Tune in to your senses

The next time you play, make a commitment to spend as much time as possible, after you have played a shot, being aware of what is going on around you. Start to really notice in detail the colours of the course, or the calming feel of the wind or, if you play on a links course, the sound of the sea. Let yourself really soak up what's going on and, as you do that, notice the effect this has on your state, on the way you feel.

We believe that this is a vital requirement for entering the zone. If you consider that in a five-hour round of golf you are only playing golf itself for about 10 per cent of the time, it seems incredible to ignore what's going on in that other 90 per cent, as though it had no bearing on how we perform. If you have the 90 per cent right you will find that the other 10 per cent starts to slot into place.

Yet have you ever had a lesson on what to do in between shots? Of course you haven't! But how could we possibly overlook the biggest chunk of our experience when playing, and render it meaningless? The amazing thing is, though, that if you ask people why they play golf they will usually say things like, 'I love being outdoors in the beautiful scenery.' 'I love the social aspect.' And, 'The course is such a peaceful place.'

All these things occur in between shots, yet in our obsession to lower our handicap and shoot lower scores we start to ignore them. Just imagine, if you can grasp the concept, that becoming more aware of what is going on around you in between shots could actually be one of the most important ingredients in helping you to shoot a lower score.

Isn't it amazing how little we actually can control out on the course? We certainly have no say in the weather, nor can we do anything about the condition of the course, the speed of the greens, or how our playing partners behave, where the golf ball goes, how it bounces, what the wind does to our shots, or the pace of play.

When you do a little analysis on this, isn't it just chaos out there? I mean, you just don't know what's going to happen. In so many areas of our lives we strive to be in control, and then we take that mindset into the game of golf and wow! doesn't that cause big problems.

Yet the paradox of all of this is that when we accept the chaos, when we accept that all sorts of strange and weird things are going to happen out there, we find that an underlying sense of order is actually present, and sense can emerge from the acceptance of the chaos.

Can control/can't control: Know the difference

If we play golf with a mindset of having to control, we will be in for some serious problems. But if we are open to all the possibilities we might encounter while playing, what emerges is an ability to perform nearer to the upper levels of our potential.

Looking at what we can actually control while playing golf, we see that there is very little – apart from our reaction to whatever the chaos throws at us. Even Tiger Woods cannot totally control where the golf ball goes. He certainly can't control the bounce of the ball and the effect of spike marks on the greens.

Normally, when people feel they have no control over a situation they experience extreme stress. This can be true of golf if you're trying to control things that are unfortunately just not under your direct influence. We are not asking you to play golf with an air of stoic resignation, but what we are putting over in the strongest way we can is the fact that you will gain more control when you accept that most of what happens out there is not under your control. The aspect that you do gain control over is the most important aspect imaginable.

Time and time again we have found that when people go through this exercise it can have a really profound effect. They realise that they have been putting so much energy into something that they cannot totally control, i.e. results, at the expense of the experience itself.

Guess what generally happens when we place our attention on the experience? The results tend to take care of themselves. Don't we see this in so many areas of our lives, as we seek answers in all the wrong places? Looking for instant results or instant thrills, each short burst of entertainment giving less and less genuine pleasure as we keep turning the notch up on the thrill meter? Isn't it true that very often it's not so much that we don't have the answer to the question, but that we haven't been able to ask the right question? So often we get stuck in a set of principles and beliefs that just keep leading us up a dead end, yet because we feel the need to hold on to old beliefs we stay stuck.

An awful lot of what this book is about is to ask you to take a look at your old golfing beliefs and really evaluate whether they are working for you and, if they are not, to enable you to replace those beliefs with something more supportive and useful.

Putting:
The game within the game

Darren: I make no apologies for devoting this final chapter entirely to the greatest of all golfing arts – putting. There can be no doubt that the scorecard will always reflect just how well the short stick has behaved.

I think I fall into the category of a streaky putter. When the birdies come they seem to arrive in flocks. I have never looked back at every scorecard I have ever returned, but I would hazard a guess that plenty would show five or six birdies in nine or 10 consecutive holes.

My childhood hero Greg Norman has always been a great putter, and there are quite a few more, American Brad Faxon included, whose ability to stroke the ball consistently into the hole I have envied. The scorecard reflects only how many strokes, not how you took them, but the key to any low round is to have as few putts as possible. Some of the concepts that Karl talks about with putting are quite revolutionary, but I do get a sense that we can help you make some big changes in the number of putts that you hole. From my own game I have found it particularly important to understand the role of the eyes in putting, and also the need to control my heart rate.

Your brain and holing putts

Karl: This section of the book applies the latest cutting-edge research on how your brain actually works with regard to rolling the ball into the cup.

It gives an understanding of the part your eyes play in making or missing those vital putts. It also shows how your beliefs will either propel you to fulfil your potential or keep you stuck in the mire of mediocrity. You will understand how the body influences the mind and vice versa. You will have an in-depth knowledge of how vital your state control is to great performance on the greens. You will understand why you have probably wasted most of your practice time up till now, and the dramatic effects that memory has on performance.

Above all, when you take in this information and finish this book, you will own a set of tools that will allow you to progress with your game in a way that will be extremely rewarding and exciting for your golfing future.

All the tools and techniques have at their root a neuroscientific basis, and a body of research, that utilises the latest findings of how the brain operates. Unfortunately, too many of the mental game programmes out in the market are full of ridiculous claims of instant transformation and enlightenment. Well, thankfully the brain doesn't work that way. You need to train your brain in much the same way that you would train your body – consistently and repeatedly. Above all, this system has been tested in the most important laboratory of all – the real world, from club golfers to Ryder Cup players and major winners. It has been proven to be effective if you use it and apply it.

But that is the key. You must take this information and digest it, think about it, and then take action, that's the absolutely critical element. If you are truly to gain some benefit from what you're about to read, then you have got to operate a bit differently from the way that most human beings do.

How can I be different?

'How do I become different?' you are probably saying to yourself. 'How can I stand out from the rest?' Human beings have a remarkable tendency that doesn't really exist in the rest of the animal kingdom. When animals perform an action such as looking for food somewhere, for instance when a monkey goes to a certain tree looking for his favourite delicacy, if he finds that that particular tree doesn't have what he wants, what does he do? He adapts his behaviour and goes elsewhere. His brain tells him to eliminate that particular tree from his enquiries. He doesn't keep going back to that tree, hoping that maybe today it just might work out if he climbs a bit higher or tries a little harder.

Yet what do human beings do in so many areas of their lives? They go to the same job every day, a job they hate, but they don't change it. They stay with the same person they don't really like, but they don't change. They keep on eating the same kind of food even though they know it is damaging their arteries. They stay on the motorway even though the signs tell them there has been an accident four junctions away, and then get stuck later in the traffic jam. They make the same resolutions to quit smoking each year, but remain smokers.

Human beings have an incredible capacity, like no other creature, to keep doing the same things over and over again, even though they don't work. Einstein said that the definition of insanity was to keep doing the same things over and over again expecting a different result. Just how many golfers are bordering on insanity in their insistence on continuing to do what doesn't work with regards to their putting?

Why is this? Well, your brain is a pattern recognition masterpiece, which means we are programmed in our genes, as a means of survival, to replicate our behaviour, to preserve our genes. This is both a wonderful piece of evolutionary programming and a complete pain in the backside when it comes to change.

The point to recognise here is that your life, where you are now, your status, your relationships, your income, your golf handicap, the number of putts you average, all are a direct result of the patterns and habits that you run, mostly unconsciously, on a daily basis.

Changing those patterns and habits needs more than just an understanding of technique; it needs an understanding of how your brain really operates, and how you can systematically go about changing some of the limiting patterns and habits that you currently run through that wonderful computer sited between your ears.

If understanding this were enough, then we wouldn't have a huge multibillion-dollar diet industry that continues to fail. Most people know these days what food is good and what's bad, yet they continue with the same patterns and habits, hoping for salvation from the very latest eating plan, much in the same way as the golfer eagerly buys his monthly golf magazine hoping to find the latest secret.

But to give you a flavour of what this is all about, let's just do a little exercise to show you what changing patterns and habits really means. Bring your hands together in front of you, slot your fingers together and have your thumbs sitting one on top of the other. Now look down at your thumbs and see which is on top. The latest research says that if your left thumb is on top of your right, then you are a highly intelligent person. If your right thumb is on top of your left, the research tells us that you are a highly sexual person. Now change the position of your thumbs around. Does that feel weird or strange?

Now fold your arms and re-fold them a different way. Some of you may even not be able to do that. What has just happened? In that very simple but profoundly important exercise I have just broken a long-standing unconscious pattern, and it felt uncomfortable and strange.

Some of the following information will have you feeling exactly the same way, a bit uncomfortable and strange. But you must always ask yourself the key question: Are my patterns and habits giving me what I truly want and deserve, or am I just running around the wheel doing a variation of the same thing, getting the same results and the same frustrations?

As I say to everybody I work with, if your patterns and habits are giving you the life you want, then please keep repeating them. I would say that Tiger Woods needs to keep repeating most of his patterns! But if your patterns are getting in the way, take some of this information that you are about to learn, and move on and progress.

Also consider what might happen if you don't do anything about this area of your game. What will happen to you as a golfer, and to the potential that you possess? What would it feel like to have played your very last game of golf? As you look back over the years and months and hundreds of rounds you may be filled with regret – regret that you had the opportunity to do something about your game, but didn't take it. You stayed the same and remained with the familiar patterns, the patterns that were certainly very comfortable, patterns that other people were running, but ultimately patterns that, as you look back over your golfing career, kept you exactly where you were, frustrated at your inability to truly experience a breakthrough.

It's not going to last forever

One of the truly extraordinary delusions that we labour under as human beings is that we are eternal and will be around for ever; but unfortunately we all have a certain number of rounds in our lifetime. We always think that things could just change tomorrow, but I promise you that they won't until you take a new direction, follow a new road map, and take action.

It's absolutely imperative that during the time we spend together we move from thinking to doing, so that you can actually, permanently, change some of the limiting patterns and habits you may have been running for so long.

You will also begin to understand that truly effective psychology is about a reduction in thought as opposed to thinking about your thinking. The game of golf is actually a physical game. It is just that we have the capacity as human beings to allow our mind to get in the way and interfere with the effective functioning of our body.

How many of you recently made a call on your mobile phone, or sent a message halfway across the world on your computer just by clicking a button and despatching an e-mail, which returned back to you in an instant with the information you needed?

What would you have done 300 years ago if you had wanted to communicate with someone even as near as your next village? You wouldn't have been able to pick up the phone and pass on your message, the postal service hadn't got into full swing then, you wouldn't be able just to jump in your car for at least another 150 years, and unless you were one of the wealthier types your horse wouldn't have had a carriage.

How did all of that change? Have you ever stopped to think, as your mobile rings once more, what kind of mindset engineered the possibility of cordless communication across the globe? Well, the mindset of 'there must be a better way than this' actually has been the catalyst for every step along the way of the communications revolution.

The mindset that involves looking at what's currently happening, and questioning whether the current way of doing things is the very best way forward – that restless mindset creates endless progress. There are some very special individuals who seek to question the norm as opposed to accepting it.

I want you to digest what I am saying, and then you may experience a mini-earthquake inside your head as some of your beliefs and ideas are challenged. When the earthquake settles you will have a tremendous opportunity for change.

Preparing to fail

The practice and preparation that you currently undertake with your putting is almost certainly a complete and utter waste of time. Have you ever stopped to think why you practise like you do, why you stand there rolling ball after ball along a putting track? Or why you stand on the green just before going out to play with three or four balls, 'trying' to hole a bunch of putts. I'll tell you why: you do it because you have been conditioned to do it, because others do it. You do it because that's the way that you're supposed to do it.

But ask yourself these questions: Has your putting got significantly better with the way that you are currently practising? Are you better now than you were when you were 16? Have you improved your skills on the greens as much as your ability on a computer, say, or your ability to drive a car, or your level of fitness? The answer for most of you I suspect is no. As a broad generalisation, most golfers' ability on the greens diminishes the longer they play the game. Not always, but in a lot of cases, the majority of you holed putts more easily at 16 than you do now.

It then rests with you to continue to do what you have always done, hoping for a different result, or to finally say 'stop, this has gone on long enough.' You take a different approach from the way you go about your practice and preparation on the greens, and finally start to roll enough putts to make significant difference to your scoring.

I would like you to think about what you do on the putting green just before you go out to play a round of golf, that 10–20 minute period I consider crucial to the way you will perform in the day ahead. Think what this time is actually all about. What purpose does this exercise actually achieve, or are you doing what we have already talked about, going through the same ritual as everybody else?

For me, the period of time that you spend on the green just prior to playing should fulfil two vital goals. You should leave the practice putting green with enhanced feel for the greens for that day, and you should have increased your confidence in your ability to hole out from short range.

If you leave the putting green with those two goals fulfilled, then you will have spent your time wisely. But is that what actually happens, or have you just spent those vital minutes going through your normal ineffective motions?

How many balls do you take on to the practice green with you? Do you take more than one? Do you roll many balls at the hole that actually miss? Do you spend a lot of time just hitting putts from 15 to 20 feet?

If you're like the majority of golfers you will probably be nodding your head in answer to those questions. And if you are, then that's great because you're almost certainly wasting your time. Why is that great? Because it gives you a tremendous opportunity to look at this particular pattern and habit, and ask yourself if it truly works, and if you actually go out with the two goals previously mentioned of increased confidence in holing out and enhanced feel.

If you don't, then you can now look to do something totally different that might just transform your scoring. After all, how many golfers go out and hit a great shot with a long iron to the first or second, and then come away with a bogey due to a three-putt, and yet after the game tend to look at what happened more towards the end of their round when they try to work out how and why shots have gone missing?

Consider the word 'feel', which is one I hear constantly during my work. 'My feel was great today,' or 'I just had absolutely no feel whatsoever.' Feel is a word that is always used, but I think that few truly understand what it means.

My definition of feel with regard to the game of golf, and specifically to putting, is the ability of your body to respond to the information given to it by your eyes.

Let's look at some examples of feel. The cricketer runs along the boundary, picks up the ball, looks at the wicket-keeper, and in an instant sends the ball into his gloves. The footballer looks up, sees a team-mate running into space, and then sends a 40-yard diagonal ball to his feet on the run. We look at the wastepaper basket, roll up a piece of paper, and throw it straight in. Our body has the ability to respond to information given by the eyes in terms of moving or throwing objects. The big difference between putting and some of the actions I have just mentioned is the green itself. The green is the critical variable in golf because, as we know, the pace of greens varies on a daily basis. The cricketer doesn't have to worry about this because the journey of the cricket ball through air doesn't have the same variables.

So if feel is about our body responding to information supplied by the eyes, and the critical variable in golf is the green, then what do we need to give our brain information about the green?

Now when you go on to the practice putting green and you send the ball to the hole, what is your brain going to be drawn towards, what will it focus on? The answer is, the hole. Every putt that you hit simply will register in the brain as in or missed; your brain is not receiving information about the critical variable which is the pace of the green. You either holed it or you didn't.

The golfer may also send one ball out, leave it short, and then respond to that ball by sending the next from the same place, adjusting slightly so it gets closer. But how many attempts at each putt do you get out on the course? If you are standing on the putting green prior to play, sending more than one ball from the same spot, you are playing bowls, not golf!

If you wish to radically improve your feel before you go out to play I would like to suggest this different approach.

NUGGET

Take one ball with you and stroke some long putts to the fringe, but with a difference. Set yourself up and take one look at the fringe, with your goal being to get the ball to rest exactly on the cut of grass. Do this each time from a completely different location, and each time that you do this your ball will either finish on, long, or short.

Then when you have done this a number of times, I want you again to set yourself up, look at the fringe, roll your ball, but without looking up you call out internally, 'Long,' 'Short,' or 'On.' Then take a look and see if your call was correct. What you are doing is putting all your sense receptors on high alert, you are truly tuning in to your feel. No longer is the goal to get the ball into the hole, which cuts off the sense of feel, the game now is to actually sense what is going on. It's like the difference between someone who knows nothing about wine, someone who just drinks red or white, and a connoisseur whose senses are finely tuned to the subtle differences in the smell and the taste of a good wine. His senses are on high alert. Putting, for most people, means their senses have been dulled to the point of being anaesthetised, because they have mixed up the goal of holing the putt with developing feel and touch.

Putt to the fringe with eyes closed to increase feel.

As you do this before you play, you are arming your brain and body with the information they need to deal with the challenges out on the course. You have an incredible piece of machinery resting between your two ears, but you have to give it clear instructions, otherwise your results will continue to disappoint.

Making the hole look bigger

What do people always say about the size of the hole when they putt well? 'It seemed like a bucket.' Or, 'I couldn't miss it.' Yet when they have a torrid time out on the greens, the hole seems to be the size of a thimble. Of course the hole doesn't actually change size, but our perceptions do.

It has often been said that 'perception is reality' – what we perceive to be true is indeed that way, no matter what anybody else thinks. Some people's perception tells them that jumping off a bridge with a piece of elastic attached to their backs is the essence of fun. It isn't my

Shape your perception; make the hole look bigger by practising to a tee.

perception, but that doesn't matter to the person enjoying the bungee jump. Our perceptions are individual, and they can change, they can be adjusted. So if our perception of the hole has some impact on our performance, shouldn't we then be doing everything in practice to shape our perception of the hole as being bigger rather than smaller?

When the golfer lines up his four balls on the green just before playing, and the first one misses, how does that register in the brain? And then the next one may go in, but the third one misses. Each miss has the potential to alter the golfer's perception for that day, before they go out to play. This unfortunately is a win/lose scenario and one that we simply cannot afford to risk.

When we miss a putt out on the course we tend to blame everything in the immediate vicinity – a poor read, a spike mark – but if you understand the brain a little more, and recognise the way it works, then some of the putts that you miss out there in the tournament may just be the result of a seed of doubt that you inadvertently sowed on the practice green.

NUGGET

Just imagine that from today you were different in that you actually took charge of how your own perceptions are being shaped. If, for instance, in the last five minutes before you set off to play, you stroked a number of eight- to five-foot putts to a tee peg, or you rolled the ball over a tiny 5p coin. Just consider what would happen at the unconscious level if you hit a putt and it just slid past the edge of the tee. How would that register in your brain in terms of a hole? As the ball just misses the tee, your mind will actually believe that the ball would have gone into the hole. But what if you hit the tee, as you undoubtedly will? How do you feel about your ability to hit such a tiny object? How big does the hole look now in comparison to your tee peg?

And what would happen out on the course if you maybe kept seeing a tee peg just behind the hole on the line you wanted to hit the ball? How do you think your mind and body would respond to such a specific target, such a small target, within the larger area of the hole? How many times would we ever actually miss a dartboard when we aimed at the bulls-eye?

Just close your eyes for a moment and bring to your mind your favourite colour. Now imagine a tee peg of that same colour and, as you do that, imagine that this tee peg is stuck in the ground on a beautiful, lush, slick green. And perhaps you could imagine a golf ball rolling towards it. Then you might see that in fact it's rolling from your putter, and this time the tee is behind the hole. As the ball rolls towards the tee, you see it being caught by the hole, and you hear the sound of the ball dropping into the hole. And you feel different because the hole just seems different, the size somehow seems to have changed.

Our ability to shape our perceptions is so vitally important in our quest to become really good on the greens. As you can now see, the period you spend before you actually go out to play can have massive implications for your results in the long term, this period of time on the practice putting green which for most people is a ritual waste of time as they do what they have always done before.

What are you scared of?

As you may have heard in relation to other areas of your life, if you do what you have always done then you'll get what you have always got.

When people discuss putting, they often talk about their fear: 'I was scared to death over that three-footer to win the match.' Or, 'My knees tremble on short putts.' If we take a closer look at what's going on here I think you may experience a truly important breakthrough.

I'm sure that most of you have experienced some form of fear out on the golf course. The question we need to ask if we have experienced this thing called fear is, what is the actual purpose of fear? What does it do for me? What is its benefit and what effect does it have on me?

Looking first at the physical effects of fear, just imagine you're playing golf on one of the most beautiful courses on earth, somewhere very special to you, somewhere spectacular and very hot, and you feel wonderful. You have just hit your ball slightly off line and are searching for it, and as you brush a path through the bushes, you catch something out of the corner of your eye. It's green, large and coiled, and your brain instantly registers danger at a snake in the grass. Your body changes its state instantly, your heart races, your palms sweat, your throat clenches, your stomach tightens, and goose pimples break out on your arms.

What on earth does this have to do with holing a putt to win a tournament? Well, your body's reaction to fear is the same whether you're faced with a real threat or an imagined one. What actually happens is that the hypothalamic-pituitary-adrenal (HPA) system in your brain releases chemical messengers, mainly dopamine and adrenaline. The HPA also triggers an outpouring of the hormone cortisol, which in turn activates a small, almond-shaped area of the brain called the amygdala. Your blood sugar and blood pressure rise steeply to give you a burst of energy, so that you can either meet the threat head on or run away from it. This is the well-known 'fight or flight' response, which is magnificent for running away from dogs and snakes, but it's deadly if you're trying to hole putts.

The brain is programmed to detect dangers, both those routinely experienced by our ancestors and those learned by us as individuals. Throughout life we add to those ancestral fears with a long list of fears that arise from our own personal life experience. Unfortunately we are not simply afraid of physical dangers such as snakes. We are afraid of any imagined situation that might evoke a painful emotion, and we run away from the perceived dangers of being failures or being ridiculed.

A new way to think

So how does that work back to our putting? Well, what are we really afraid of? And how can we possibly hope to move our bodies with a smooth stroke if we have the same chemicals coursing through it as we would if we had just seen a snake?

Now consider something quite radical and different: we are never afraid to miss a putt, or to send a white ball towards a small hole. What we are actually afraid of is the feeling we get as a result of the consequence of missing. We are afraid of feeling bad because our brain registers this as dangerous. Yet how do we try to protect ourselves from this? By mechanics, or working on our stroke. But how effective is that? No matter how technically perfect our stroke is, we are still going to miss a lot.

This is why stroke breakdown occurs – because you have got a couple of million years of evolutionary tools telling you to avoid this situation, to be frightened of it. Add in a few comments from TV such as, 'He is faced with a terrifying three-footer to win,' and your brain quite naturally will go on full-tilt red alert saying 'Avoid!'

So how do we deal with this massively important situation? The old-fashioned school of positive thinking would have you go out believing that you will hole putts. That would be fine if it worked. If by thinking positively you could go out and hole everything, then great, but unfortunately it doesn't seem to work that way, does it? We can't totally control whether a golf ball goes into the hole or not because there are just too many variables, and no amount of positive thinking can overcome that. Paradoxically, for most people positive thinking often has the opposite effect. It actually creates fear and anxiety at a subtle level because, having thought positively but missed, what do you do now?

Just imagine an alternative, that before you went out to play you made a commitment to deal with the outcome of any putt out on the course, a heartfelt commitment that whatever ills and misfortunes you suffered, you would commit to dealing with them. If we accept that we will deal with the worst that can happen before we play, as opposed to hoping for the best, then we are strangely set free. If a golfer is not afraid to lose, then he is not afraid to win.

This is not thinking negatively, it is accepting reality. But the acceptance that you are prepared to deal with, to overcome, the worst that can happen, changes the meaning of the situation in your brain. Suddenly a four-foot putt is not a snake in the grass, it's more like a branch of a tree that you once took for a snake. You have seen through the illusion, and your brain will now perceive differently, allowing you to function, and that stroke you spent so many hours perfecting now has the opportunity to come out to be set free, as opposed to being shackled by an illusionary fear.

More than just technique

The whole concept of what you are going to do when you're actually on the putting green has been discussed and analysed many times. Normally the discussion hinges on the kind of stroke you might use, the way that you set up, the way to read greens, or even the actual putter that you choose.

In this section I am going to set before you some systems and research that haven't been presented anywhere before, but which are based on scientific discoveries of how the mind, body and even the heart interact, to determine whether your ball goes into the cup or not.

Imagine something you're frightened of, something which, just by thinking about it, starts to make you feel uneasy. It may be having to speak in front of 1,000 people and then forgetting your lines, or sitting in the dentist's chair when you start to hear the buzz and whine of the drill, or breaking down in your car at midnight in a neighbourhood that you just don't want to be alone in at that time, or a snake slithering its way into your room.

As you allow your mind to go to something that frightens you, just notice how the very act of running those thoughts through your mind can make you start to feel differently. You may feel a little tension creeping into your muscles. You may even detect that your heart has started to beat a little faster. Your mind just seems to be a little bit more scrambled than before

Now just try to imagine what it would be like to try to hole some very important putt when in this state. How would you feel about that now? The thoughts that run through our minds profoundly influence the way we feel, but have you ever stopped to consider that your heart rate will profoundly influence your ability, first, to see the line of a putt and, secondly, to judge the pace?

Heart and mind are inextricably linked. Whatever is happening in your head influences your heart rate, and by the same measure the way that your heart beats dramatically affects your thought patterns. Consider a time in your life when you may have felt panicky – a racing heart and a distracted, disturbed, racing mind go hand in hand.

Most psychological systems attempt to give you techniques of thought control that will hopefully allow you to control your body better. This is often difficult to do out on the course in the heat of battle. I have found it to be of massive benefit to have tools and techniques available to you whereby you can control your mind through the body. These are practical systems that have been proven to be effective out on the course, not just in a theory session in a classroom.

Body and mind working as one

Some fascinating insights into how the body and mind work together have come to light through the extraordinary work and research done at the HeartMath Institute in the USA (www.heartmath.com). With this in mind I want you to consider a fascinating subject called entrainment.

Entrainment is a situation where all the major systems in the body come together in synch, the major systems being the heart, the brain, and the respiratory system.

In the 17th century, a Dutch physicist by the name of Christiaan Huygens took great pride in the invention of the pendulum clock. He maintained a fine collection of such clocks in his studio. One day he noticed a very peculiar phenomenon: all the clocks' pendulums were swinging in unison even though they hadn't started out that way.

He then stopped the clocks and re-started them, swinging the pendulums at different rhythms. To his amazement, all the pendulum clocks soon fell back into synchronisation again. Every time he misaligned their swing, they fell back into synch.

Huygens couldn't solve the problem, but later scientists did: the largest pendulum – the one with the strongest rhythm – was pulling the other pendulums into synch with it. This phenomenon, known as entrainment, has been found to be prevalent throughout nature.

When the body is in entrainment, its major systems work in harmony. Your biological systems operate at higher efficiency because of that harmony, and as a result you think and feel better.

Because the heart is the strongest biological oscillator in the human system – the equivalent of the largest pendulum – the rest of the body's systems can be pulled into entrainment with the heart's rhythm. This state of head/heart entrainment occurs precisely when the heart rhythms complete one cycle every ten seconds (0.1Hz). When brain waves entrain with heart rhythms at 0.1Hz, the research suggests this is the optimal state to enter the zone and produce peak performance.

According to scientific studies at the Institute of HeartMath research, at those elusive moments when we transcend our ordinary performance and feel in harmony with something else – whether it's a glorious sunset, inspiring music, or another human being – what we are really coming into synch with is ourselves. Not only do we feel more relaxed and at peace at such moments, but the entrained state also increases our ability to perform well and offers numerous health benefits. In entrainment, we're at our optimal functioning capacity.

Taking theory to the course

You may be wondering what all this has got to do with holing more putts and getting your scores down. Maybe an awful lot more than you might think. As most people walk on to the putting surface, especially after a good shot, or if they see the ball resting close enough to the flag so that they feel they should hole the putt, the thoughts that are running through the mind start to have an effect on the heart rate. Usually, their thought patterns start to send the heart, mind and body out of synch.

The ability to hole the putt is being reduced from the moment they walk on to the putting surface, and all the great ideas about how they should stroke the ball, the pre-shot routines, the green-reading systems etc, will have little or no impact because they are simply not in the optimum state to hole the putt: body and mind are working against each other, and to try to do something about it during the putting routine is way too late.

When we are in our heads 'thinking', it's difficult to be in our bodies, yet it is the body that plays golf, it is a physical game with a physical club. When we have our attention in our body, we are much more able to perform, to allow putts to be sunk, and great shots to emerge. One of the detrimental effects of sports psychology is that many golfers are now thinking about their thinking, which is no better than the previous generation's obsession with thinking about their swinging.

When we have our attention more in the body, we actually enter that strange place called the 'present moment', which for most golfers, and for that matter most people in the western world, is an alien place. We have been almost culturally conditioned to mind-hop constantly from the past to the future. A very wise man once said, 'All of the wisdom that we will ever need we will find in the present moment.'

But to be in the present moment we have to be present to something that is actually happening now. The body is in the now. Think of it this way: is it possible to project your body into the future? Well unless you have some form of time machine available it obviously isn't possible, and yet how easily does the mind create scenarios of future possibilities, and then dwell on past occurrences. Our body, not our mind, is the gateway to the now.

I think this concept has such profound implications for us all because it is almost a western disease to be in our heads, 'thinking' all the time, and while we think it is so difficult to be or do anything.

NUGGET

What I want you to do specifically with your putting is to consider the green itself almost like a separate place from the rest of the golf course, just like the wicket is separate from the field in cricket, or the penalty area in football is separate from the rest of the pitch. As you walk on to the green I want you to perform a very specific but massively important ritual each time you 'enter the ring', so to speak.

As you walk on to the green I want you each time to look down at the fringe, and then look up. As you look up I want you to place your attention in your heart area. Now, with your attention in your heart area I want you to imagine that you are 'breathing through your heart' – literally imagine that you are breathing through your heart area. Do this for a number of seconds as you walk on to the green. When you do this, a number of extremely important functions will be taking place simultaneously. First, as you breathe through your heart you will be actively slowing down your heart rate at a very subtle level, and as you do this you will create the opportunity for mind and body to come into synch, to go into entrainment.

As you go into entrainment your ability to read the line, visualise the line, and feel the putt, will increase dramatically. You will also be taking your attention away from your racing mind and putting it back into your body, the place where you are actually going to perform the action to hole the putt.

Misaligned? The eyes have it

Researchers in the field of putting have often pointed out that most golfers misalign when they putt, and I tend to agree with this. But if we consider for a moment what we actually have to do to hole a putt, it comes down to some very simple tasks. We first of all have to pick a line that the ball will travel on into the hole, feel the pace of the putt, and then we need to set the ball off on the correct line.

Now if we pick the correct line when we read the putt, but never aim ourselves correctly along that line, how on earth can we ever expect to hole more than a few fluky putts? In fact if we don't line up correctly the only time we should actually hole a putt is when we have totally misread it. But surely we can't be that bad at lining ourselves up? Surely we have been provided with some evolutionary tools to send us in a given direction?

I have spent some considerable time researching the role of the eyes in putting. After long discussions with some leading experts in the field I asked the question, 'When we look at the line of a putt as we read the green, what is actually happening?' I was told that, basically, as we crouch down to read a green, our eyes take a kind of Polaroid snap of the line to the hole. The clearer we keep this Polaroid snap, the less distortion we give it, the greater the chance we have of holing the putt.

So what is it that most golfers do wrong in this critical period from taking the Polaroid snap of the line to then setting up and misaligning?

Before we consider what's happening on the greens, let me ask if you would agree that a rifle is a reasonably good instrument in setting the bullet out on the line that you intend? If you aim the rifle correctly, chances are you will hit the target. What would happen, though, if you tried to hit the target with your rifle if you stood with the gun held out to your side at arm's length? Picturing this ridiculous scenario you realise that your image of the target would be severely distorted unless you lined the rifle up with the sights in your eye-line so that the target, you, and the gun, were all in line.

Most golfers pick their line, walk up to the ball, and set up for a practice stroke at the side of the ball. This is like firing a rifle held out to your side. If you do this, you are in effect taking another, different, Polaroid of the line that you intend to send the putt on. But why do we do this? We do it because everyone else is doing it, even though it doesn't make any sense. For me, one of the single most important patterns you can change with your putting is to take your practice stroke from behind the ball but in line with your target, or dispense with the practice stroke altogether. Remember, the clearer and less disturbed your Polaroid is of the line you intend, the easier and more efficiently will you roll the ball out on that intended line. This is all about allowing the information supplied by your eyes to your brain and then back to your body to be as clear and undiluted as possible.

With a really clear picture of the line, you are providing your brain with a very precise piece of information which it will work with beautifully if you let it. You will actually feel that you're doing things quite a bit more quickly – but if this worries you, ask yourself how many more putts do you hole when you take longer to pull the trigger?

Also, perhaps we need to consider what purpose or value there is in a practice stroke. For me there's obvious value in a practice stroke for full shots, because you're trying to key into your brain a complex set of motor movements before you play the shot. The putting stroke, by contrast, is in essence not a great physical challenge in terms of co-ordination in the way that a 250-yard drive would be. But perhaps we should consider the other point usually given for the practice stroke, which is to get some feel for the length of putt.

Inbuilt feel and touch: trusting your on-board computer

At this stage I think we need to take something of a leap of faith, and trust in a mechanism we have within us that can judge distance incredibly well. We could go out on to the putting green now, and if I stood four feet away from you and asked you to throw a ball at me, you would do it perfectly. I could then move to 10 feet and you would do the same, 14 feet the same, and so on.

You would do this totally unconsciously; you would just look and react. But if I asked you to take a practice throw before each attempt, the chances are that your accuracy would diminish, you would get in your own way. So why do we think that having practice strokes before a putt should actually help us? We do it because everybody else does; but the more we trust our unconscious ability to judge distance, the more we get out of our head and into the body, the more we let go. It seems to me that we then allow ourselves to putt with a freedom that so many of us had as youngsters, but which somehow got conditioned out of us as we got older and supposedly smarter, and we started to think and analyse instead of to react. The system is incredibly efficient if you just allow the eyes to take the Polaroid. This gives the mind-body system the information it needs, and then you can allow the body to react beautifully.

It's almost a case of 'Stop thinking and come to your senses'. So much great putting is about the absence of thought and the presence of feel. But feel doesn't come from mental processing; it comes from getting out of your own way and allowing your intelligence to take over your body as opposed to your conceptual knowledge.

To allow that intelligence to take over, we need to be in a certain state, a state of calm which you will find you can experience more and more as you follow these guidelines, start to link mind and body together, get out of your own way, and develop the mindset that releases your true potential.

Great putting is certainly far more about imagination and creativity than mechanics. Don't think I'm saying mechanics aren't important; they obviously are, and it's great to have a good putting stroke. But over the years I have seen so many golfers with great-looking strokes who don't hole a thing. You do need to develop the mechanics of your game, but then undertake to commit to the suggestions in this programme so as to allow those mechanics to flourish, rather than let yourself be trapped into thinking you can create the theoretically perfect stroke that will never let you down. It doesn't exist, and never has. But what does exist is an incredibly developed evolutionary system between your ears that can judge distance, aim at things, and perform tasks remarkably well, but first you have to recognise this, then create the conditions for it to flourish, and then just allow it to operate.

The 'in-between' of putting

Now we should consider the 'in-between'. As we have already seen, a massive part of the game is the time spent on the golf course when you aren't actually playing golf – 90 per cent of your time on the course you are doing something else.

This in-between time is of course almost completely overlooked in conventional coaching. Most golf lessons take place out on the driving range or putting green, where there is no interval between shots, no time lapse between one shot and the opportunity to correct that fault with the next ball.

But what you do during this 'in-between' time will be the critical element in your search to become a better player. What you do with your mind and body during this time will almost certainly determine the quality of your performance during your actual play.

To look at this area and do something constructive about it takes a leap of faith. You can't analyse it in the way you analyse a swing flaw, you can't actually touch it. It's intangible, and we human beings find intangibles hard to deal with. We would much rather place our attention on something that everybody else is doing, namely mechanics, something we can see and grasp hold of.

The vast majority of people think that what they are doing during the 'in-between' is concentrating or focusing. Let me put that straight, because what they aren't doing is concentrating; what they're actually doing is worrying. They're burning up vast reserves of mental energy by allowing their minds either to dwell on past mistakes or project themselves into an imagined future.

Our minds can be in one of only three places in terms of time. If I asked you to think about the best holiday that you have had in the last five years, your mind would take you into the past. If I asked you to consider what you will be doing on Christmas Day this year, your mind will transport you into the future. And as I talk with you now and ask you to place your focus on your breathing, your mind is residing in the present.

With just those three options available to us at any one time, we can become clearer on the fact that all the mental danger on the golf course exists in the past and the future. It's pretty unlikely that you have ever got really angry about something that hasn't happened yet, or that you have got nervous over something that has already occurred. Once you have hit that first tee shot, nerves tend to quieten, because we generally only get nervous about something we predict will happen in the future.

The really negative emotions of anger and anxiety do reside in different places – past and future – and the mind is just brilliant at flipping those two switches and taking us away from our present experience.

Staying in the 'now'

A remark we often hear commentators make is, 'All he has to do is stay in the present, don't let his mind wander.' This is great advice, but it's a little like saying, 'Just speak Japanese' – very easy if you are Japanese and know how, but impossible if you aren't and don't.

As we have already pointed out, it's obviously possible to time-travel with our minds, but not with our bodies, unless you have available some kind of tardis or time machine. So it's the body that potentially becomes a gateway for us, an opening for us to be in the present moment. When we are in our body we are in the moment, and when we are in the moment in sport we have the potential to play way above our normal standard. There's an expression, 'He played out of his mind,' which usually describes a peak performance. Well, if you're not in your mind where are you? In your body.

Think of some of the many activities that we do to relieve stress and to feel good: we go running, we dance, we have a hot bath or a sauna, we do yoga - all these kinds of activities tend to take us out of our minds and place us back in touch with our bodies.

This all works in a really interesting circle of excellence, because the more we are in our body, the more we reside in the moment, the calmer and better we feel. And that allows performance to occur.

So the time in between shots offers you one of two opportunities. You can either burn up lots of mental energy, fretting about future shots or outcomes, getting even more angry about shots you've already played; or you can spend some time residing in the body, allowing your mind to be calm, and actually conserve the mental energy that will be so crucially important for the rest of the round.

Well, how on earth do I get into my body, you're probably asking. There are a number of options here, but I have found a couple to be extremely successful over my years with players at all levels of the game.

NUGGET

One way that we can actually re-connect with our body and the present moment is through our walking. During every round of golf you play, I would like you to take some time in between shots to actually focus your attention on the feeling of the ground under your feet. Just set out with the intention that on each hole you will spend a short few strides feeling the texture of the grass, the pace that you walk, the length of your stride, how you are actually moving your body. Just hold your attention on this simple motion that you do every single day of your life, which is something that you normally do without paying any conscious attention to it.

As you do this seemingly ridiculous drill, you will be enjoying some extraordinary benefits at a subtle level of your mind. Placing your attention on the walk, you will be literally grounded into the present moment, you will be entering the magic of 'now', and as you go into 'now' your mind learns to be still and quiet, and you get away from that incessant chatter inside your head and back to a place of calmness.

As you give yourself this mental break you will be actually replenishing your mental energy level, and creating an environment that will allow relaxed focus on the next putt you hit.

Scoring your mental game

Now, for the next six rounds of golf that you play I want you to keep another form of score – and this will be a score out of 18. If you score 12 out of 18 it will mean that on 12 of the holes you were able to spend some time focusing on the feeling of the ground under your feet. Your goal of course is to score 18 out of 18, and I guarantee that if you work with this for six rounds, and you keep score each time, you will at the very least come off the course with more energy and less burnout. That's the booby prize, the least you can expect. On the plus side, you may just find that your mental state is such that you seem to be holing a few more putts.

Another very important technique I want you to work with during the in-between time concerns your eyes. It has been proved beyond any doubt that when we are uptight and agitated our eyes tend to dart around inside our head as we are processing our agitated thoughts. But the more the eyes dart around the more agitated we become, and of course the more agitated we become the less likely will we be to succeed in any aspect of our game, let alone on the putting surface. The opposite is also true: 'quiet' eyes can create a quiet mind. As our eyes become still our mind tends to follow.

Eyes up!

As you walk down the fairway, I want you first of all to try and keep your eyes above the level of the flag. Contrast this with most golfers who are having a bad day with their heads sunk in their chests. The position of our eyes has a profound influence on how we feel. When our eyes are down we tend to access the part of the brain that is involved with self-talk and feelings – not a good place for a golfer to be. Some of the phrases we use in everyday life give a clue to this aspect. For instance, when somebody is feeling a little blue we tend to say, 'She's looking a bit down.' Well, she is – quite literally. When things seem to be on the mend and times are happier then 'things are looking up'.

With your intention of keeping your eyes above the level of the flag, you will automatically be changing the way that you feel. As you do this, allow your eyes to relax, giving yourself a command to 'relax the eyes'. Things tend to go out of focus, but you feel different, and you may notice that your breathing has changed. You may also notice that you feel more relaxed generally. As your eyes go soft, still, and de-focused, you will be literally changing the way that you think and feel as you bring the mental chatter into a calm state, a state conducive to peak performance.

We all know that the state of mind that we are in on any given shot will pretty much decide the outcome of that shot, but we give little or no thought to how that particular mindset has been caused or constructed. Yet our habitual thought patterns and habits during the 'in-between' time will, I promise you, be the key difference in your pursuit of golfing fulfilment.

Technique will never protect you from poor shots. I was recently questioned by a non-golfer, who asked me a question so simple that it could only have come from someone who didn't actually play the game, someone who hadn't been hypnotised like the rest of us into believing certain myths about what you should and shouldn't do. What he said was, 'How do you get to be a good golfer? What do you have to actually do? Is it all in the technique or is there more to it than that?'

I thought for a moment and then answered that, for me, getting better at golf was all about hitting more good shots and reducing the amount of bad shots.

'Does technique do that for you?' he asked. I replied that good technique would definitely increase the amount and quality of good shots you hit because of the basic laws of physics that govern the game.

'So good technique stops you hitting bad shots?' he asked. It was a simple question but profound, because as I began to answer, it hit me hard that no amount of work on technique will ever totally protect me from playing bad shots.

No one who has played this game has, or ever will, play without missing some putts or hitting some poor shots. We absolutely have to develop the tools and mindset that allow us to cope with those inevitable poor shots, and this coping with the poor shots usually is required in the 'in-between' time.

Yet how many golfers practise all their lives in the hope of finding a technique so strong, so good, that they will never have to deal with a poor shot? What an incredible illusion! We will never get there, and while we have that mindset we will never totally focus our minds on developing the ability to deal with poor shots – and that's what it is, an ability. Once a person has complete confidence in his ability to deal with and get over poor shots, he is not afraid of them so much. If we aren't afraid of failure because we know we can deal with it, then all of a sudden we are not afraid to succeed. Technique may always allow us to play better shots, but it will never ever protect us totally or insure us against poor shots. So we have to develop the skills of mental toughness, and train our brains to allow us constantly to deal with the inevitable chaos that we will encounter on the course.

Off the course: how those missed putts will affect you

As we have already seen, our brain stores information rather like a computer, so that every time you go out on to the golf course your brain will file that experience called golf. Now in terms of what happens on the green, your brain will store all of the putts that you have either holed or missed. But it is how you store those experiences that will tremendously influence your future performance and self-belief.

Tiger Woods has gone on record as saying that the key to the mental game is the ability to instantly recall success and to purge yourself of failure. Yet most people do the exact opposite – they have great difficulty in replicating success, and they tend to hang on to failure. This is very much down to your brain, how you store your experiences, and how your memory either shapes your future in the way you wish, or condemns you to repeating constantly the same old patterns and habits.

Emotional memories

I want you to do a little experiment with me now: think of your most embarrassing golf shot ever. How long ago was that, and how vivid is your recall?

Now I want you to think about the fourth hole that you played six rounds ago. How vivid is that? How easily can you recall it?

For most of you, the first memory will have been instantly recalled, even though the hole you hit the shot on was possibly played a number of years ago. You probably re-experienced it very clearly in pictures, sounds and feelings. But how did you get on with recalling the shot on the fourth hole, just six rounds ago? For most people, this will probably be quite vague, if you can remember it at all.

Something quite remarkable is going on here. I have basically asked you to recall just two golf shots from your golfing library of experience; one of them you could recall instantly; the other you probably had to dig quite hard to retrieve. Yet they were just two shots from your personal history.

The difference between the two – one instantly recalled, the other with difficulty – is all about emotion. In the world of psychology we are only just beginning to scratch the surface on the effects of emotion on memory and learning, but for a golfer or sportsperson the findings are of massive importance.

As we explained earlier, a memory with an emotional attachment to it will be much more easily recalled. This of course makes perfect sense. We can all remember what we were doing when we saw the events of 9/11 unfold in front of our eyes. Those images are burned into our memory, and for many are far too easy to recall.

So what if emotion does play such a role in our memory and learning, what has that got to do with our putting? Perhaps everything. Some fascinating research by one of the world's leading experts on memory, Elizabeth Loftus, is beginning to suggest that we need not be bound up to the effects of the past, and that our memories can be shaped and possibly even altered. A cornerstone of Loftus's research findings is the effect that an emotional attachment has on the recall of a particular memory.

We all want to have more good days on the greens, and reduce the amount of poor days. We all want consistency, which is a habit – a memory stored in the brain that just keeps repeating over and over again. But if memory is so profoundly influenced by emotion, how can we do something about this?

You have to change and be different from the collective mindset of the rest of the world. You have to opt out of the world mindset that creates tremendous neural connections to failure but does little or nothing actively to influence the future predictability of success.

Misery loves company

What do golfers tend to talk about after a round, even if they have played well? Very often, it's the putting. 'I played great,' you might hear, 'but I missed such an easy putt on 16.' And not only do golfers want to talk about it, it's also the *way* they talk about it: 'That three-putt on nine was a disaster.' 'I definitely choked on that short one on 17.' 'The putting felt awful today.'

We are also conditioned at a subtle but very effective level to think that good putting is somehow bad. How many times have we been part of the conversation that goes, 'He got it round in 68 – but he holed everything,' said in a tone that would almost suggest some form of cheating. How many times have we heard a player say almost with an air of self-congratulation, 'I knocked it on 15 greens out there, but three-putted six times.'

We tend to put massive emotion into putting badly, but little or no emotion into the great putts that we have holed.

Now consider this piece of information and digest it with every ounce of your being!

> **NUGGET**
>
> Every time you put emotion into a missed putt, every time you call a three-putt a disaster, every time you glow with pride at three-putting five times, you are saying at the unconscious level of your brain, 'Brain repeat, brain repeat, brain repeat.' By the way that you process those experiences in your mind you are increasing your ability to recall those failures again. You are simply using emotion to prove yourself a failure.

If you don't want to dwell in this totally ineffective and wasteful mindset, then let's start to utilise emotion and memory to enhance our performance as opposed to hinder it.

Look at three key areas – *language*, *reaction*, and *review*.

Mind your language

For the next week, monitor the language you use with regard to your putting; go into observer mode. Because most of the patterns we have are totally unconscious, we have no idea about how badly we speak of ourselves. What I want you to do in particular with your language is to notice whether you use two of the most damaging forms of self-talk, that is language which is permanent and personalised.

Consider statements such as, 'I am the worst putter in the world,' or, 'I always miss those three-footers when I really need them,' or, 'I have no feel whatsoever.' These statements are influencing you massively at a level of your psyche that you're not even aware of. Said often enough, and with sufficient intensity, these statements create an identity. You may have heard the saying that you become what you think about most, but I believe a truer statement would be that you become what you talk about most. As you constantly repeat statements to yourself your brain will act in a very literal way. It is almost as if the brain just keeps storing the statements it takes in, and builds an ever more unshakable belief in your inability to hole putts.

Think of it this way. We have heard the research that suggests for every cigarette a person smokes it will take a certain number of seconds or minutes off their life. Well, every permanent or personalised negative statement you make about your ability with the putter will result in another missed putt, somewhere, sometime. It's like a bank account. If you start out wealthy, but constantly take money from the account without ever replacing any of it, your wealth soon turns into poverty.

Just take a moment to recall in your mind now some recent event where you putted badly. What did you say to yourself as you missed the putts? What did you say afterwards to yourself, to others? As you notice this, just be aware of the permanent and personalised nature of what you said.

Please don't think for one minute that I am asking you to become some kind of weird Pollyanna, an always positive person who never grumbles but keeps a permanent smile on his face while racking up yet another three-putt. That's just plain ridiculous. What I am asking you to do is to change the way that you speak to yourself and others.

Two very different statements about the same result are: 'There wasn't much of a roll on that one;' and, 'My stroke felt a bit iffy on the back nine today.' But as you can see, neither of them is permanent or personalised.

This may seem to you almost irrelevant, but I cannot stress enough the importance of monitoring the way that you talk to yourself and others when things don't go to plan. This doesn't just apply in golf, it takes in the whole of your life.

As we have seen, the psychologist Dr Martin Seligman has contributed a significant body of research on what he calls 'explanatory style', i.e. how you explain to yourself the events in your life, good or bad, and how this will basically provide the key to your enjoyment, well-being and effectiveness in life. He has dedicated his life's work to the study of optimism and pessimism, and his research findings bear out overwhelmingly the fact that when all things are equal, i.e. talent and ability, the optimistic person will win every time.

How does he define an optimistic person? Someone who is super-positive all the time? Absolutely not. Dr. Seligman has long argued that 'false' positivity has little or no effect. What we are looking for is the ability to think non-negatively in the face of life's upsets. In other words, we can explain bad events to ourselves in a temporary and detached way, such as, 'We just put some poor strokes on it today,' and not, 'I am the worst in the world, etc.

Taking charge of your self-talk is one of the greatest challenges that we can undertake, but one with the most profound benefits. Working with putting is very useful in that it's very specific to one small area of your life. Make the commitment now first of all to monitor your talk about your ability on the green, and after you have monitored it for a while, and probably been shocked at how bad it is, then take the steps to change. You will find that change in such a small area could spread to many other areas of your life. Not that I am suggesting that you become an optimist as opposed to a pessimist in all areas. That would be too much to do. Goodness, you might even start to enjoy life!

Reaction

Now consider reaction. Remember the way that the brain works – the more emotion you put into something the more enhanced the memory, and the more enhanced the memory the more chance you have of repeating the cycle. We need to increase massively the emotion on your good putts, and decrease your emotion on the bad putts.

Now am I suggesting that when you hole a four-foot putt for a par that you put your golf shirt over your head and dance around the green? No, I'm not suggesting any massive outward show – a fist pump or a clenched fist is fine – but what I do want is massive internal emotion. As you walk off the green after holing a good putt, I want you to say inside three times, 'Yes, Yes, Yes!' Just imagine that now as you walk off the green. Your whole neurology lights up as you say internally those three yeses. Each time you do this you're creating a neurological link in your brain that is telling your mind-body system, 'Brain repeat, brain repeat.' As you do this time and time again, your whole identity as a putter will begin to be re-shaped.

On the down side you're probably thinking, 'This stuff is fine when I hole a few, but what happens when I miss the inevitable short putt, or waste a perfectly good three iron into the middle of the green by taking three more to get down?' Of course this will happen, but it's your reaction to it that is so important, remembering the golden rule of decreasing the emotion on a negative outcome.

When we experience a negative emotion such as anger after a missed put, we will also experience a corresponding reaction in terms of our physiology. Our breathing patterns will change along with our body language. A show of anger isn't necessarily the most destructive thing that can happen to us; it's what we do next that will count in the long run. Will we recover? Or will we set off on that spiral of negativity that all too rapidly can go totally out of control? If you think of any round you have played, you will find that there is usually one critical point during the round when one bad shot leads to a series of other bad shots. It may be the first of the day, but one shot can lead to a host of others.

To have control over this in your putting involves a very powerful technique with your breath which has been proven to be effective at the very highest levels of the game.

The most important point here is that you have to take action, you have to commit, follow through, and create a new pattern. So for the next 10 rounds that you play I want you to keep another score on your card. After each hole you will place a tick or a cross at the side of the hole - a tick will signify that you have either said 'Yes, Yes, Yes!' after holing a putt, or you have taken the 'Ssshhhh breath' to clear the air. If you didn't do one or other of the two you will place a cross against the hole number.

Your goal is obviously to score 18 out of 18, but you will find that at first you don't manage this. However, if you do this for 10 rounds you will have a new habit and pattern that could transform not only your putting, but your whole game.

NUGGET

Most people attempt to control their state by taking a couple of deep breaths, the attention being on breathing in to get rid of any negativity and reduce the emotional charge. This is completely ineffective. What you need to focus on after missing a putt is actually getting rid of all the air in your lungs. As you do this you will metaphorically be letting go and purging the negative emotion at the same time. This is called the 'Ssshhhh breath'.

Now look up and imagine that you're facing someone who is 20 yards away, and you are going to say 'Ssshhhh!' to them very quietly – but you're going to say this until there is absolutely no air whatsoever left in your lungs. Ready – 'Ssshhhh!'; keep going – 'Sssshhhh!' – and then take in a full, deep, abdominal breath. Notice how you feel different, how you change your posture and how you feel a release. This is such a simple but effective means to let go of negativity and move on.

Now commit to taking a 'Ssshhhh breath' every time you walk off the green if the outcome has been anything less than the one you wanted. Make that commitment now. In effect, you will walk off every green doing one of two things. If you have holed a putt, you will walk off to the tune of 'Yes, Yes, Yes!' inside your head as you create that neurological link in your brain that says, 'Do that again.'

If you happen to miss, or you just have a standard two-putt, you will walk off the green with the 'Sssshhhh breath' as you allow the emotion to release, and the very least you will get is a levelling of your emotion as opposed to the downward spiral. Isn't it strange that when we get over a problem we say we have 'cleared the air'? This is exactly what you're doing for yourself as you walk off the green, instead of the normal pattern, which is to beat yourself up, get emotional, and at a subtle level increase the likelihood of this mistake occurring again.

Review: learning not dwelling

Finally we get to 'review'. How can you ensure that your memories of the day's events on the golf course will actually enhance your future performance? One of the key points I want to make is the difference between learning from a mistake and dwelling on it. One involves growth, the other is a possible road to destruction. If we go back to our previous analogies about the brain storing experience like a computer or video recorder, we can explain the difference between learning and dwelling.

If you imagine that your last round of golf is now stored in video format in the theatre of your mind, you have the option of sitting down and watching the performance again. As you do this, pay attention to the mistakes you made, but make sure you're watching this in a kind of detached fashion, as though it was someone else you were viewing. As you view this from a distance, your mindset is one of 'What can I learn from this so that I can make progress in the future?' With your mind focused in this way you watch the video with a sense of emotionless purpose. You are like a doctor looking at the x-rays of a patient's broken leg, not the patient himself, screaming at the pain. With this mindset you will be able to take the learning and move on as you let go of the emotional attachment.

This is very different from just passively sitting and replaying the poor performance over and over again until you get to the point of feeling really miserable. This has no benefit other than massively increasing the likelihood of the poor outcome occurring again, but it is the way that most of us have been conditioned, to sit and replay in our mind the mistakes that we have made.

Of all the techniques we have talked about, this 'reviewing' is probably the most advanced and challenging, but with potentially the greatest rewards. This is the difference between a good mind and a champion mind. A champion learns and then moves on, while most of the rest of us dwell on the poor performance, and the more we dwell the more we stay stuck at the same level. It is so important, not just for putting out, but for our lives in general, that we develop the ability to finish as many days as possible on a good note so that we can keep moving towards our goals and ambitions.

NUGGET

One final aspect that I would like you to commit to is to begin a logbook. This will contain the results that you have obtained from some of the other techniques we have discussed but, most importantly, every time you play golf you should note down a detailed description of the best putt that you have hit that day. You don't necessarily have to have holed the putt, but you must describe in detail your thoughts and emotions prior to, during, and after you hit the putt.

You might write, 'I looked at the line and immediately my mind was made up about the line I was going to take.' 'I felt a sense of certainty in my body as I got set.' 'I'd told myself of the possibility of this one, and at the same time knew that I had the capability to deal with the outcome.' 'Holding the putter felt very good in my hands.' 'The stroke just flowed.' 'A nice sweet sound as the ball left the club face.' 'As I glanced up, the ball was tracking perfectly along my line.' 'In it went – that felt tremendous.' 'More confirmation.' 'I thought of the progress being made.'

How does that make you feel, as you now consider what may be ahead of you when you make a strong commitment and say yes to the programme you have just enjoyed, and the future in front of you as you develop into the golfer that you know deep down you are capable of becoming?

Conclusions

Darren: What I have always found particularly helpful and beneficial is the simplicity of Karl's research, theories and suggestions, as I am sure you will have too. Hopefully we will have been able to send you out towards lower scores and greater enjoyment of the great game that is golf. The importance of having goals and aspirations to play great golf, but not at the expense of enjoying the here and now, has become particularly apparent to me. We both sincerely hope that you have enjoyed reading this book, and have gained some valuable insights into becoming more of what you want to be as a golfer.

We will leave you with a couple of final thoughts. We have discussed many important issues that will allow you to hole more putts on the green. You now understand far more about how your brain operates with regard to sending the ball towards the hole. You know that you need to take action and that you have to do things to make a difference. But what does the future actually hold for you with the putter in your hand? What does the future hold for you as a golfer, or indeed as a person?

A new future

Karl: If we think a little more about the agitated state of mind most people live with on a daily basis, and the fact that descriptions of peak performance in sport almost always propose a calm and peaceful mind, perhaps we need to look at our inbred western mindset of always striving, pushing, wanting to be there rather than here.

If we consider that our mind and our thinking can only be in one of three places – past, present or future – how much time do you actually spend being totally present to your experience? Maybe you are at this very moment totally present to the experience of reading this book, or maybe you are half-reading. Maybe your mind is already well into the future and how you will be able to change, or maybe you're reading the book but thinking about what you have to do at work today, or booking your next tee time at the club, or the next tournament. Or perhaps you're the type of person who looks at life with a backward glance: 'What if things had been different?' 'What if I hadn't missed that putt?' 'If only I could have two-putted that day.' If only, if only. Our mind has a remarkable capacity to rob us of the present moment because we are always thinking. Yet the only moment we can ever truly experience, the only moment we can ever really be with, is the here and now.

Now stop what you are doing and just for a couple of seconds be aware of your thoughts. Notice and observe them. Notice how your mind moves very swiftly from one thought, or idea, or concept, to another, and then another. Simply pay attention to the fact that your thoughts do indeed come and go. That's the nature of thought, it's temporary because it is here and then it's gone. What most of us do is become victims of our thoughts. We get wrapped up in them, we believe them, and as we spend so much time in our heads, thinking, we leave little or no room for just doing and allowing.

The essence of great sport is creativity and spontaneity, while happiness is actually an absence of thought. We encourage you to become more and more absorbed in the here and now, be with whatever it is that you are doing whether it be holing a putt, hitting a shot, having a conversation on the phone, or eating a meal. Make a commitment to be present, to be fully into the experience, and be curious about how much of your attention has previously been sprayed around everywhere.

As you become totally absorbed in the moment of holing the putt, realise that this is the place where your mind desperately longs to be. Your desire to win, to improve, and all of that, is a result of being here and now, being in this moment.

As you become more aware of the fact that holing putts, hitting great shots, and enjoying life in general, is about this moment, then you will want to go there more and more. The activity will become a pleasure in and of itself rather than an activity to get you something, or to make you something.

Ultimately we are not looking for a positive or negative mind – the state that will allow so much is the state of calm, and that arises from the present moment. Nearly all the exercises and tools you have found in the preceding pages are gateways to the experience of the moment. The more you use them the more you will enjoy them and the more they will become your normal state of mind. That state of mind will allow you to be as good as you can be, but most importantly it will allow you to gain pleasure along the way in actually finding out and exploring what you are truly capable of.